Flinn Scientific
ChemTopic™ Labs

Solubility and Solutions

Senior Editor

Irene Cesa
Flinn Scientific, Inc.
Batavia, IL

Curriculum Advisory Board

Bob Becker
Kirkwood High School
Kirkwood, MO

Kathleen J. Dombrink
McCluer North High School
Florissant, MO

Robert Lewis
Downers Grove North High School
Downers Grove, IL

John G. Little
St. Mary's High School
Stockton, CA

Lee Marek
Naperville North High School
Naperville, IL

John Mauch
Braintree High School
Braintree, MA

Dave Tanis
Grand Valley State University
Allendale, MI

FLINN SCIENTIFIC INC.
"Your Safer Source for Science Supplies"
P.O. Box 219 • Batavia, IL 60510
1-800-452-1261 • www.flinnsci.com

ISBN 1-877991-80-5

Copyright © 2003 Flinn Scientific, Inc.

All rights reserved. No part of this book may be reproduced or transmitted in any form or by any means, electronic or mechanical, including, but not limited to photocopy, recording, or any information storage and retrieval system, without permission in writing from Flinn Scientific, Inc.
No part of this book may be included on any Web site.

Reproduction permission is granted only to the science teacher who has purchased this volume of Flinn ChemTopic™ Labs, Solubility and Solutions, Catalog No. AP6368 from Flinn Scientific, Inc. Science teachers may make copies of the reproducible student pages for use only by their students.

Printed in the United States of America.

Table of Contents

	Page
Flinn ChemTopic™ Labs Series Preface	i
About the Curriculum Advisory Board	ii
Solubility and Solutions Preface	iii
Format and Features	iv–v
Experiment Summaries and Concepts	vi–vii

Experiments

Factors Affecting Solution Formation	1
It's in Their Nature	13
Solubility and Temperature	25
Preparing and Diluting Solutions	39
Freezing Point Depression	51

Demonstrations

Aloha Chemical Sunset	63
Solutions, Colloids, and Suspensions	65
Alka-Seltzer® and Gas Solubility	69
Sorting Out Solutions	73
Instant Hand Warmers	75

Supplementary Information

Safety and Disposal Guidelines	78
National Science Education Standards	80
Master Materials Guide	82

Flinn ChemTopic™ Labs Series Preface
Lab Manuals Organized Around Key Content Areas in Chemistry

In conversations with chemistry teachers across the country, we have heard a common concern. Teachers are frustrated with their current lab manuals, with experiments that are poorly designed and don't teach core concepts, with procedures that are rigid and inflexible and don't work. Teachers want greater flexibility in their choice of lab activities. As we further listened to experienced master teachers who regularly lead workshops and training seminars, another theme emerged. Master teachers mostly rely on collections of experiments and demonstrations they have put together themselves over the years. Some activities have been passed on like cherished family recipe cards from one teacher to another. Others have been adapted from one format to another to take advantage of new trends in microscale equipment and procedures, technology innovations, and discovery-based learning theory. In all cases the experiments and demonstrations have been fine-tuned based on real classroom experience.

Flinn Scientific has developed a series of lab manuals based on these "cherished recipe cards" of master teachers with proven excellence in both teaching students and training teachers. Created under the direction of an Advisory Board of award-winning chemistry teachers, each lab manual in the Flinn ChemTopic™ Labs series contains 4–6 student-tested experiments that focus on essential concepts and applications in a single content area. Each lab manual also contains 4–6 demonstrations that can be used to illustrate a chemical property, reaction, or relationship and will capture your students' attention. The experiments and demonstrations in the Flinn ChemTopic™ Labs series are enjoyable, highly focused, and will give students a real sense of accomplishment.

Laboratory experiments allow students to experience chemistry by doing chemistry. Experiments have been selected to provide students with a crystal-clear understanding of chemistry concepts and encourage students to think about these concepts critically and analytically. Well-written procedures are guaranteed to work. Reproducible data tables teach students how to organize their data so it is easily analyzed. Comprehensive teacher notes include a master materials list, solution preparation guide, complete sample data, and answers to all questions. Detailed lab hints and teaching tips show you how to conduct the experiment in your lab setting and how to identify student errors and misconceptions before students are led astray.

Chemical demonstrations provide another teaching tool for seeing chemistry in action. Because they are both visual and interactive, demonstrations allow teachers to take students on a journey of observation and understanding. Demonstrations provide additional resources to develop central themes and to magnify the power of observation in the classroom. Demonstrations using discrepant events challenge student misconceptions that must be broken down before new concepts can be learned. Use demonstrations to introduce new ideas, illustrate abstract concepts that cannot be covered in lab experiments, and provide a spark of excitement that will capture student interest and attention.

Safety, flexibility, and choice

Safety always comes first. Depend on Flinn Scientific to give you upfront advice and guidance on all safety and disposal issues. Each activity begins with a description of the hazards involved and the necessary safety precautions to avoid exposure to these hazards. Additional safety, handling, and disposal information is also contained in the teacher notes.

The selection of experiments and demonstrations in each Flinn ChemTopic™ Labs manual gives you the flexibility to choose activities that match the concepts your students need to learn. No single teacher will do all of the experiments and demonstrations with a single class. Some experiments and demonstrations may be more helpful with a beginning-level class, while others may be more suitable with an honors class. All of the experiments and demonstrations have been keyed to national content standards in science education.

Chemistry is an experimental science!

Whether they are practicing key measurement skills or searching for trends in the chemical properties of substances, all students will benefit from the opportunity to discover chemistry by doing chemistry. No matter what chemistry textbook you use in the classroom, Flinn ChemTopic™ Labs will help you give your students the necessary knowledge, skills, attitudes, and values to be successful in chemistry.

About the Curriculum Advisory Board

Flinn Scientific is honored to work with an outstanding group of dedicated chemistry teachers. The members of the Flinn ChemTopic Labs Advisory Board have generously contributed their proven experiments, demonstrations, and teaching tips to create these topic lab manuals. The wisdom, experience, creativity, and insight reflected in their lab activities guarantee that students who perform them will be more successful in learning chemistry. On behalf of all chemistry teachers, we thank the Advisory Board members for their service to the teaching profession and their dedication to the field of chemistry education.

Bob Becker teaches chemistry and AP chemistry at Kirkwood High School in Kirkwood, MO. Bob received his B.A. from Yale University and M.Ed. from Washington University and has 16 years of teaching experience. A well-known demonstrator, Bob has conducted more than 100 demonstration workshops across the U.S. and Canada and is currently a Team Leader for the Flinn Foundation Summer Workshop Program. His creative and unusual demonstrations have been published in the *Journal of Chemical Education*, the *Science Teacher*, and *Chem13 News*. Bob is the author of two books of chemical demonstrations, *Twenty Demonstrations Guaranteed to Knock Your Socks Off, Volumes I and II*, published by Flinn Scientific. Bob has been awarded the James Bryant Conant Award in High School Teaching from the American Chemical Society, the Regional Catalyst Award from the Chemical Manufacturers Association, and the Tandy Technology Scholar Award.

Kathleen J. Dombrink teaches chemistry and advanced-credit college chemistry at McCluer North High School in Florissant, MO. Kathleen received her B.A. in Chemistry from Holy Names College and M.S. in Chemistry from St. Louis University and has more than 31 years of teaching experience. Recognized for her strong support of professional development, Kathleen has been selected to participate in the Fulbright Memorial Fund Teacher Program in Japan and NEWMAST and Dow/NSTA Workshops. She served as co-editor of the inaugural issues of *Chem Matters* and was a Woodrow Wilson National Fellowship Foundation Chemistry Team Member for more than 11 years. Kathleen is currently a Team Leader for the Flinn Foundation Summer Workshop Program. Kathleen has received the Presidential Award, the Midwest Regional Teaching Award from the American Chemical Society, the Tandy Technology Scholar Award, and a Regional Catalyst Award from the Chemical Manufacturers Association.

Robert Lewis teaches chemistry and AP chemistry at Downers Grove North High School in Downers Grove, IL. Robert received his B.A. from North Central College and M.A. from University of the South and has more than 26 years of teaching experience. He was a founding member of Weird Science, a group of chemistry teachers that has traveled throughout the country to stimulate teacher interest and enthusiasm for using demonstrations to teach science. Robert was a Chemistry Team Leader for the Woodrow Wilson National Fellowship Foundation and is currently a Team Leader for the Flinn Foundation Summer Workshop Program. Robert has received the Presidential Award, the James Bryant Conant Award in High School Teaching from the American Chemical Society, the Tandy Technology Scholar Award, a Regional Catalyst Award from the Chemical Manufacturers Association, and a Golden Apple Award from the State of Illinois.

John G. Little teaches chemistry and AP chemistry at St. Mary's High School in Stockton, CA. John received his B.S. and M.S. in Chemistry from University of the Pacific and has more than 36 years of teaching experience. Highly respected for his well-designed labs, John is the author of two lab manuals, *Chemistry Microscale Laboratory Manual* (D. C. Heath), and *Microscale Experiments for General Chemistry* (with Kenneth Williamson, Houghton Mifflin). He is also a contributing author to *Science Explorer* (Prentice Hall) and *World of Chemistry* (McDougal Littell). John served as a Chemistry Team Leader for the Woodrow Wilson National Fellowship Foundation from 1988 to 1997 and is currently a Team Leader for the Flinn Foundation Summer Workshop Program. He has been recognized for his dedicated teaching with the Tandy Technology Scholar Award and the Regional Catalyst Award from the Chemical Manufacturers Association.

Lee Marek retired from teaching chemistry at Naperville North High School in Naperville, IL and currently works at the University of Illinois—Chicago. Lee received his B.S. in Chemical Engineering from the University of Illinois and M.S. degrees in both Physics and Chemistry from Roosevelt University. He has more than 31 years of teaching experience and is currently a Team Leader for the Flinn Foundation Summer Workshop Program. His students have won national recognition in the International Chemistry Olympiad, the Westinghouse Science Talent Search, and the Internet Science and Technology Fair. Lee was also a founding member of Weird Science and has presented more than 500 demonstration and teaching workshops for more than 300,000 students and teachers across the country. Lee has performed science demonstrations on the *David Letterman Show* 20 times. Lee has received the Presidential Award, the James Bryant Conant Award in High School Teaching from the American Chemical Society, the National Catalyst Award from the Chemical Manufacturers Association, and the Tandy Technology Scholar Award.

John Mauch teaches chemistry and AP chemistry at Braintree High School in Braintree, MA. John received his B.A. in Chemistry from Whitworth College and M.A. in Curriculum and Education from Washington State University and has 26 years of teaching experience. John is an expert in microscale chemistry and is the author of two lab manuals, *Chemistry in Microscale, Volumes I and II* (Kendall/Hunt). He is also a dynamic and prolific demonstrator and workshop leader. John has presented the Flinn Scientific Chem Demo Extravaganza show at NSTA conventions for eight years and has conducted more than 100 workshops across the country. John was a Chemistry Team Member for the Woodrow Wilson National Fellowship Foundation program for four years and is currently a Board Member for the Flinn Foundation Summer Workshop Program. John has received the Massachusetts Chemistry Teacher of the Year Award from the New England Institute of Chemists.

Dave Tanis is Associate Professor of Chemistry at Grand Valley State University in Allendale, MI. Dave received his B.S. in Physics and Mathematics from Calvin College and M.S. in Chemistry from Case Western Reserve University. He taught high school chemistry for 26 years before joining the staff at Grand Valley State University to direct a coalition for improving pre-college math and science education. Dave later joined the faculty at Grand Valley State University and currently teaches courses for pre-service teachers. The author of two laboratory manuals, Dave acknowledges the influence of early encounters with Hubert Alyea, Marge Gardner, Henry Heikkinen, and Bassam Shakhashiri in stimulating his long-standing interest in chemical demonstrations and experiments. Continuing this tradition of mentorship, Dave has led more than 40 one-week institutes for chemistry teachers and served as a Team Member for the Woodrow Wilson National Fellowship Foundation for 13 years. He is currently a Board Member for the Flinn Foundation Summer Workshop Program. Dave received the College Science Teacher of the Year Award from the Michigan Science Teachers Association.

Preface
Solubility and Solutions

Solubility, the ability of one substance to dissolve in another, is an important part of chemistry—in the lab, in the environment, and in the body. Many chemical reactions are carried out in solution in order to control the concentrations of reactants and the rates of reactions. In nature, minerals dissolve in lakes and streams, where they may affect the survival, growth, and reproduction of aquatic organisms. Dissolved ions in the bloodstream regulate nerve transmission and energy production. The purpose of *Solubility and Solutions*, Volume 12 in the Flinn ChemTopic™ Labs series, is to provide high school chemistry teachers with laboratory activities that will help students investigate the principles and properties of solutions. Five experiments and five demonstrations allow students to study the factors that affect solution formation, the nature of solute–solvent interactions, and the concentration and composition of solutions.

Solutes and Solvents

Understanding how reaction conditions will affect the rate at which a solute dissolves in a solvent can help students build a conceptual model of solution formation. In "Factors Affecting Solution Formation," an inquiry-based activity, students design a series of tests to determine the effects of the crystal size of the solute, the temperature of the solvent, and the mixing of the solution. In "It's in Their Nature," students examine the solubility patterns of ionic, polar, and nonpolar compounds in a variety of solvents. The results allow students to classify compounds and to understand how solute–solvent interactions influence both the solubility of a pure substance and the energy involved in forming a solution. The remarkable strength of solute–solvent interactions is dramatically illustrated in the demonstration "Sorting Out Solutions." As the size of the dissolved or dispersed particles in a solution changes, so do the properties of the mixture. In the demonstration "Solutions, Colloids, and Suspensions" students observe how these mixtures are distinguished from one another based on the size characteristics of the dispersed particles—their settling behavior, diffusion through a membrane, and ability to scatter light.

Solubility and Saturated Solutions

The solubility of a solute depends on temperature. The most common solute used in solubility curve determinations is potassium nitrate, whose solubility increases more than 1700% as the temperature increases from 0 to 100 °C. "Solubility and Temperature" is a unique, microscale-based adaptation of the classic solubility curve experiment involving potassium nitrate. Graphical analysis of the results allows students to determine at a glance whether a solution is unsaturated, saturated or supersaturated. If heat is absorbed when a solute dissolves, then the reverse process, when a solute recrystallizes from solution, should release heat. This lesson is readily apparent in "Instant Hand Warmers," an applied chemistry demonstration, where students learn to appreciate the chemistry behind the "instant heat—any place, any time" guarantee. Finally, in "Alka-Seltzer® and Gas Solubility," students learn that generalizations are not always valid and that the effect of temperature on the solubility of a gas may be different than what they might predict.

Solution Concentration and Composition

Preparing and analyzing accurate concentrations of solutions is an important skill in the chemistry laboratory. The technology-based experiment "Preparing and Diluting Solutions" gives students the opportunity to develop this key analytical skill as they prepare their own solutions and investigate the relationship between the concentration of a solution and its absorbance. Many properties of a solution, the so-called colligative properties, depend not only on the concentration of a dissolved solute, but also on the number of particles that are formed in solution when the solute dissolves. In "Freezing Point Depression," students measure the freezing point depression obtained for a variety of solutes and correlate the results with the concentration and composition of the solution.

Safety, Flexibility, and Choice

Depend on Flinn Scientific to give you the information and resources you need to teach chemistry safely and effectively. The selection of experiments and demonstrations in *Solubility and Solutions*—combined with complete sample data and teachers notes—encourages and empowers every teacher to find "solutions" that will help reach their students, in their classrooms, and using their resources. Each experiment and demonstration in *Solubility and Solutions* has been thoroughly tested and retested. You know they will work! Use the experiment summaries and concepts on the following pages to locate the concepts you want to teach and to choose activities that will help you meet your goals.

Format and Features

Flinn ChemTopic™ Labs

All experiments and demonstrations in Flinn ChemTopic™ Labs are printed in a 10⅞" × 11" format with a wide 2" margin on the inside of each page. This reduces the printed area of each page to a standard 8½" × 11" format suitable for copying.

The wide margin assures you the entire printed area can be easily reproduced without damaging the binding. The margin also provides a convenient place for teachers to add their own notes.

Concepts — Use these bulleted lists along with state and local standards, lesson plans, and your textbook to identify activities that will allow you to accomplish specific learning goals and objectives.

Background — A balanced source of information for students to understand why they are doing an experiment, what they are doing, and the types of questions the activity is designed to answer. This section is not meant to be exhaustive or to replace the students' textbook, but rather to identify the core concepts that should be covered before starting the lab.

Experiment Overview — Clearly defines the purpose of each experiment and how students will achieve this goal. Performing an experiment without a purpose is like getting travel directions without knowing your destination. It doesn't work, especially if you run into a roadblock and need to take a detour!

Pre-Lab Questions — Making sure that students are prepared for lab is the single most important element of lab safety. Pre-lab questions introduce new ideas or concepts, review key calculations, and reinforce safety recommendations. The pre-lab questions may be assigned as homework in preparation for lab or they may be used as the basis of a cooperative class activity before lab.

Materials — Lists chemical names, formulas, and amounts for all reagents—along with specific glassware and equipment—needed to perform the experiment as written. The material dispensing area is a main source of student delay, congestion, and accidents. Three dispensing stations per room are optimum for a class of 24 students working in pairs. To safely substitute different items for any of the recommended materials, refer to the *Lab Hints* section in each experiment or demonstration.

Safety Precautions — Instruct and warn students of the hazards associated with the materials or procedure and give specific recommendations and precautions to protect students from these hazards. Please review this section with students before beginning each experiment.

Procedure — This section contains a stepwise, easy-to-follow procedure, where each step generally refers to one action item. Contains reminders about safety and recording data where appropriate. For inquiry-based experiments the procedure may restate the experiment objective and give general guidelines for accomplishing this goal.

Data Tables — Data tables are included for each experiment and are referred to in the procedure. These are provided for convenience and to teach students the importance of keeping their data organized in order to analyze it. To encourage more student involvement, many teachers prefer to have students prepare their own data tables. This is an excellent pre-lab preparation activity—it ensures that students have read the procedure and are prepared for lab.

Post-Lab Questions or Data Analysis — This section takes students step-by-step through what they did, what they observed, and what it means. Meaningful questions encourage analysis and promote critical thinking skills. Where students need to perform calculations or graph data to analyze the results, these steps are also laid out sequentially and in order.

Format and Features
Teacher's Notes

Master Materials List — Lists the chemicals, glassware, and equipment needed to perform the experiment. All amounts have been calculated for a class of 30 students working in pairs. For smaller or larger class sizes or different working group sizes, please adjust the amounts proportionately.

Preparation of Solutions — Calculations and procedures are given for preparing all solutions, based on a class size of 30 students working in pairs. With the exception of particularly hazardous materials, the solution amounts generally include 10% extra to account for spillage and waste. Solution volumes may be rounded to convenient glassware sizes (100-mL, 250-mL, 500-mL, etc.).

Safety Precautions — Repeats the safety precautions given to the students and includes more detailed information relating to safety and handling of chemicals and glassware. Refers to Material Safety Data Sheets that should be available for all chemicals used in the laboratory.

Disposal — Refers to the current *Flinn Scientific Catalog/Reference Manual* for general guidelines and specific procedures governing the disposal of laboratory waste. Because we recommend that teachers review local regulations before beginning any disposal procedure, the information given in this section is for general reference purposes only. However, if a disposal step is included as part of the experimental procedure itself, then the specific solutions needed for disposal are described in this section.

Lab Hints — This section reveals common sources of student errors and misconceptions and where students are likely to need help. Identifies the recommended length of time needed to perform each experiment, suggests alternative chemicals and equipment that may be used, and reminds teachers about new techniques (filtration, pipeting, etc.) that should be reviewed prior to lab.

Teaching Tips — This section puts the experiment in perspective so that teachers can judge in more detail how and where a particular experiment will fit into their curriculum. Identifies the working assumptions about what students need to know in order to perform the experiment and answer the questions. Highlights historical background and applications-oriented information that may be of interest to students.

Sample Data — Complete, actual sample data obtained by performing the experiment exactly as written is included for each experiment. Student data will vary.

Answers to All Questions — Representative or typical answers to all questions. Includes sample calculations and graphs for all data analysis questions. Information of special interest to teachers only in this section is identified by the heading "Note to the teacher." Student answers will vary.

Look for these icons in the *Experiment Summaries and Concepts* section and in the *Teacher's Notes* of individual experiments to identify inquiry-, microscale-, and technology-based experiments, respectively.

Experiment Summaries and Concepts

Experiment

Factors Affecting Solution Formation—An Inquiry-Based Approach

Solutions of copper sulfate, an important agricultural chemical, are sprayed on grapes and wheat and many other plants to prevent fungus diseases. What factors will affect the rate at which copper sulfate dissolves in water? In this inquiry-based experiment, students must design a series of tests to investigate how changing the crystal size of the solute, the temperature of the solvent, or the mixing of the solution will affect the rate at which copper sulfate dissolves. The results help students understand how and why solutions form.

It's in Their Nature—Solute–Solvent Interactions

"Oil and water do not mix." This old saying is often used as a metaphor to explain why relationships between opposites are difficult or almost impossible. In this experiment, students trace this metaphor back to its source—the nature of oil and water, solutes and solvents, and the interactions between them. By studying the solubility patterns of ionic, polar, and nonpolar compounds in a variety of solvents, students learn to classify compounds and begin to understand the types of intermolecular attractive forces that exist between them.

Solubility and Temperature—A Solubility Curve

Potassium nitrate is the classic solute used in solubility curve determinations—its solubility in water increases an incredible 1700% from 0–100 °C! The purpose of this microscale experiment is to construct a solubility curve for potassium nitrate in water by measuring saturation temperatures for six different solution concentrations. Graphical analysis of the data allows students to determine at a glance whether a solution is unsaturated, saturated or supersaturated.

Preparing and Diluting Solutions—Concentration and Absorbance

Solutions are an important part of chemistry. But how are accurate concentrations of solutions prepared? In this technology-based experiment, students practice analytical techniques as they prepare and dilute a series of copper sulfate solutions of known molarity. They then investigate the relationship between the concentration and absorbance of the solutions and use this information to determine the accuracy of their calculations and their technique.

Freezing Point Depression—How Low Can You Go?

People who live in northern states are familiar with winter and the snowy, icy roads that go with the season. Road crews spread salt and other deicing chemicals on the roads in order to lower the temperature at which freezing occurs. What solutes will have the greatest effect on the freezing point of a solution? Is it possible to cool an ice-water mixture to almost –20 °C using just sodium chloride? In this introduction to colligative properties, students measure the freezing point depression for four different solutes and learn how the concentration and number of dissolved solute particles affect the freezing point of water.

Concepts

- Solution
- Solubility
- Solute
- Solvent

- Solute and solvent
- Polar vs. nonpolar
- Intermolecular forces
- Miscibility of liquids

- Solubility
- Saturated solution
- Saturation temperature
- Solubility curve

- Concentration
- Molarity
- Dilution equation
- Absorbance

- Freezing point
- Freezing point depression
- Colligative property
- Molality

Flinn ChemTopic™ Labs — Solubility and Solutions

Experiment Summaries and Concepts

Demonstration

Concepts

Aloha Chemical Sunset—Colloids and Light Scattering

Watch as the sun sets over a chemical reaction! The reaction of sodium thiosulfate with hydrochloric acid produces elemental sulfur, which precipitates from solution to form a colloidal mixture. When the reaction is carried out on an overhead projector, the light from the projector is scattered by the colloidal sulfur particles and produces a multicolored chemical "sunset."

- Colloid
- Light scattering
- Tyndall effect

Solutions, Colloids, and Suspensions—Principles and Properties

Solutions, colloids, and suspensions are defined and distinguished from one another based on the size characteristics of the dispersed particles. Are the particles large enough that they will settle upon standing or be trapped by a filter? Are the particles small enough that they will pass through a semi-permeable membrane? What size particles will scatter light that is passed through the mixture? Learn all about the principles and properties of mixtures using this comprehensive demonstration.

- Solution
- Colloid
- Light scattering
- Semipermeable membrane

Alka-Seltzer® and Gas Solubility—Effect of Temperature

Our students' understanding of chemical principles is shaped by what they see or feel in the real world. For the effect of temperature on solubility, students often will generalize from their everyday experiences preparing food and beverages and conclude that substances are more soluble at higher temperatures. In the case of gases, however, this generalization is always wrong! Let's see what an Alka-Seltzer tablet can teach us about the effect of temperature on the solubility of a gas.

- Gas solubility
- Reversible reactions
- Thermal pollution

Sorting Out Solutions—Hydrogen Bonding Demonstration

The total is not always equal to the sum of the parts! Use this two-part demonstration to highlight the effect of hydrogen bonding and other intermolecular forces on the properties of solutions. If you mix 50 mL of glycerol and 50 mL of water, the volume of the resulting solution should be 100 mL, right? Wrong! Although water and many alcohols are miscible, their solutions have a smaller volume than the original liquids. Add an ionic solute to an alcohol solution, however, and watch as the solution separates itself into two layers.

- Miscible liquids
- Hydrogen bonding
- Salting-out

Instant Hand Warmers—Supersaturated and Saturated Solutions

Instant heat—any place, any time! Instant hand warmers contain a supersaturated solution of sodium acetate. A supersaturated solution is inherently an unstable (non-equilibrium) condition. When the solution is "stressed," the dissolved solute seems to come crashing out of solution, releasing lots of heat in the process. The mixture gets so hot, it "freezes"! Use this discrepant event demonstration to teach your students about solubility, crystallization, and heats of solution.

- Saturated solution
- Supersaturated solution
- Crystallization
- Exothermic reaction

Teacher Notes

Factors Affecting Solution Formation
An Inquiry-Based Approach

Introduction

Copper sulfate, a crystalline blue solid that readily dissolves in water, is an important agricultural chemical. In solid form the compound is mixed into animal feeds to prevent copper deficiency in farm animals. Solutions of copper sulfate are sprayed on plants, including wheat, potatoes, tomatoes, grapes, and citrus fruits, to control fungus diseases. Although copper sulfate is soluble in water, the rate at which it dissolves can be fast or slow, depending on conditions. What factors affect the rate at which an ionic solid dissolves in water?

Concepts

- Solution
- Solubility
- Solute
- Solvent

Background

A solution is a mixture of two or more pure substances that is homogeneous or uniform throughout. The substance that is being dissolved is called the solute, and the substance that does the dissolving is called the solvent. Solubility, defined as the amount of solute that will dissolve in a given amount of solvent at a particular temperature, depends on the nature of the solute and the solvent and how they interact. Although the solubility of a compound governs how much solute may dissolve, it does not predict how fast the solute will dissolve. Some of the factors that may affect the rate at which a solid will dissolve in a liquid are the particle size of the solid, the temperature of the solvent, the amount of stirring or agitation of the mixture, how much solute is already dissolved in the solvent, and the presence of other dissolved solutes.

The process of an ionic solute dissolving in water is a surface phenomenon. Free-moving water molecules randomly collide with ions on the surface of the solid. The water molecules interact with the ions by means of ion-dipole attractive forces and gradually "chip" away at the surface ions, helping to separate them from the bulk crystal. As the surface ions dissolve, the next layer of ions becomes the new surface layer. This interaction at the surface of a crystal continues until the crystal is completely dissolved or until the solution can accept no more solute.

Understanding the way in which an ionic solute dissolves can help us design conditions to optimize the rate at which the solid dissolves.

Experiment Overview

The purpose of this inquiry-based activity is to investigate the effects of crystal size, degree of mixing, and temperature on the rate at which copper(II) sulfate pentahydrate ($CuSO_4 \cdot 5H_2O$) dissolves in water.

The widespread use of copper sulfate as an agricultural chemical may give the false impression that it is not toxic. Copper sulfate is toxic to humans and many other organisms. It is precisely because of its toxicity that copper sulfate is an effective fungicide, algaecide, and herbicide.

Factors Affecting Solution Formation – Page 2

Pre-Lab Questions

1. Use the "surface model" described in the *Background* to predict how changing each of the following variables will change how fast a crystalline ionic compound dissolves in water: (a) amount of stirring or agitation; (b) temperature of water; (c) size of the crystals.

2. Outline a series of tests to determine how each variable will affect the rate at which copper(II) sulfate pentahydrate dissolves in water. Each test should look at the effect of changing only one variable at a time—all of the other variables must be controlled or held constant for comparison.

3. Read the *Materials* section and the recommended *Safety Precautions*. Write a step-by-step procedure for the experiment, including any safety precautions that must be followed. *Note:* There are two crystal sizes of copper sulfate. Use about 0.2 g of the fine crystal grade as the control variable. Fill the test tubes about one-third full with distilled or deionized water.

Materials

Copper(II) sulfate, $CuSO_4 \cdot 5H_2O$, fine crystals, 1–2 g
Copper(II) sulfate, $CuSO_4 \cdot 5H_2O$, crystal lumps, 0.2 g
Distilled or deionized water
Ice
Balance, centigram (0.01 g) precision
Beakers, 100-mL, 2
Graduated cylinder, 10- or 25-mL
Hot plate or hot water
Mortar and pestle
Spatula
Stirring rod (optional)
Stoppers to fit test tubes, 3 (optional)
Test tubes, large, 3
Test tube clamp
Test tube rack
Thermometer
Timer
Weighing paper or dishes

Safety Precautions

Copper(II) sulfate is moderately toxic by ingestion and is a skin and respiratory tract irritant. Avoid contact with skin and eyes. Wear chemical splash goggles and chemical-resistant gloves and apron. Wash hands thoroughly with soap and water before leaving the laboratory.

Procedure

1. Verify the procedure with your instructor and review all safety precautions.
2. Carry out the procedure and record all data in a suitable data table.
3. Answer the following *Post-Lab Questions*.

Teacher Notes

For a more challenging lab environment, add an element of competition to this inquiry activity. Give teams a goal—to prepare 50 mL of 0.1 M copper(II) sulfate by having the solid dissolve in 30 seconds or less!

*Page 3 – **Factors Affecting Solution Formation***

Teacher Notes

Post-Lab Questions

1. What effect did mixing or shaking have on the rate at which the solute dissolved in water? Give specific evidence from your tests and explain in terms of the "surface model" for solution formation.

2. How did increasing the temperature of the solvent change the rate at which copper sulfate dissolved in water? Was the opposite effect observed when copper sulfate was dissolved in cold water?

3. Use the definition of temperature and the kinetic theory to explain the effect of temperature on the rate of solution formation for copper sulfate.

4. In some cases, increasing the temperature may be a disadvantage in preparing a solution. Suggest a possible case where heating the solution might be a problem.

5. What was the effect of crystal size on the rate of dissolving? How do these results support the surface model for solution formation?

6. Use the results of this experiment to predict how the rate of dissolving would be affected if you tried to dissolve more copper sulfate in a solution that already contained some copper sulfate rather than in distilled water. *Note:* Assume that the total (combined) amount of solute is less than the solubility limit of copper sulfate.

7. Write a short paragraph describing an optimum procedure for preparing a solution.

For many of these questions, it may help students to draw pictures of what they think is happening at the level of ions and molecules.

Teacher's Notes
Factors Affecting Solution Formation

Master Materials List *(for a class of 30 students working in pairs)*

Copper sulfate, $CuSO_4 \cdot 5H_2O$, fine crystals, 25–30 g	Spatulas, 15
Copper sulfate, $CuSO_4 \cdot 5H_2O$, crystal lumps, 2 g	Stirring rods, 15 (optional)
Distilled or deionized water	Stoppers to fit test tubes, 45 (optional)
Ice	Test tubes, 20 × 150 mm, 45
Balances, centigram (0.01 g) precision, 3	Test tube racks, 15
Beakers, 100 mL, 10*	Test tube clamps, 15
Graduated cylinders, 10- or 25-mL, 15	Thermometers, 15
Hot plates or hot water, 5*	Timers or clock
Mortars and pestles, 5*	Weighing paper or dishes, 75

*Several groups may share hot plates, ice baths, and mortars and pestles.

Safety Precautions

Copper(II) sulfate is moderately toxic by ingestion (LD_{50} 300 mg/kg) and is a skin and respiratory tract irritant. Avoid contact with skin and eyes. Wear chemical splash goggles and chemical-resistant gloves and apron. Remind students to wash their hands thoroughly with soap and water before leaving the laboratory. Please consult current Material Safety Data Sheets for additional safety, handling, and disposal information.

Disposal

Consult your current *Flinn Scientific Catalog/Reference Manual* for general guidelines and specific procedures governing the disposal of laboratory waste. The test solutions may be rinsed down the drain with excess water according to Flinn Suggested Disposal Method #26b.

Lab Hints

- The laboratory work for this experiment can be completed in one 50-minute lab period if students are well prepared in advance of lab. The *Pre-Lab Questions* may be assigned to help students plan their tests and to lead a class discussion before students begin work in the lab. To ensure a safe lab environment, it is essential that the teacher check the students' procedures and their understanding of the necessary safety precautions, as recommended in the *Procedure*.

- The value of an inquiry-based activity is in allowing students to try different approaches and to learn from their mistakes. To save time and still derive this value from the experiment, the lab may be designed as a collaborative group activity by assigning different tests to different groups of students. Each group should be responsible for reporting both on their approach to the tests and on their results.

- Copper sulfate pentahydrate is available in four different solid forms: powder, fine crystals, medium crystals, and large crystalline lumps. As mentioned in the *Pre-Lab,* we recommend using the fine crystal grade (reagent grade, Flinn Catalog No. C0102) as the control. Depending on what form(s) you have in your storeroom, however, you can modify this

The copper sulfate solutions may be collected and saved for repeat or alternative use. Copper sulfate solutions may be used, for example, to demonstrate colorimetry and to illustrate complex-ion and single replacement reactions.

Teacher's Notes

Teacher Notes

recommendation to suit your needs. Thus, if only the medium crystals or large crystalline lumps are available, students may be instructed to grind the crystals to obtain small crystals for use as a control and a fine powder for use in particle size testing. Laboratory grade material may give different results than reagent grade material and may not give completely clear solutions. Do not use anhydrous copper(II) sulfate.

- Let students take the initiative in deciding on appropriate controls for how solutions should be mixed and how the rate of dissolving should be measured. Students will find that it is not practical to choose "no mixing" as the control because it takes too long for the samples to dissolve. They might decide to measure the "rate" of dissolving not in terms of time but in terms of the number of times a test tube must be swirled, shaken or "flicked" in order to get the solid to dissolve.

- In order to investigate how fast a solid dissolves, students can measure the amount of time required to dissolve a solid completely or they can compare the color of the solution and/or the amount of solid that has dissolved after a certain period of time. In looking at the effect of mixing, students may choose to stir the solutions, invert or shake the test tubes a certain number of times, swirl the test tubes for a certain period of time, etc. Students will get the most out of this "simple" experiment if they have enough time to try out different approaches to these problems and see what approach gives them the most information.

- See the *Supplementary Information* section for a sample procedure and sample data tables. These may be used as an alternative student handout, if desired.

Teaching Tip

- Use the results of this experiment to help students predict the relative solubility of different solutes in different solvents and the energetics of solution formation. The basic premise in the surface model for an ionic solute dissolving in water is that polar water molecules interact with ions on the surface of the solid. What happens if solute particles do not interact with solvent molecules or do not interact as strongly as solvent molecules interact with each other? Energy is always required to pull apart solute particles from the surface of a crystal lattice. Energy is also required to overcome attractive forces among solvent molecules and "expand" the solvent to make room for solute particles. Energy is released when solvent molecules interact with solute particles. The relative contribution of these energy terms helps explain why many water-soluble, ionic compounds nevertheless have positive heats of solution. In these cases, dissolving a solid is favored by entropy. The effect of the favorable entropy contribution increases with increasing temperature. (Recall, $\Delta G = \Delta H - T\Delta S$.)

Dissolving solids that have positive heats of solution is an excellent example to use when introducing the ideas of entropy and free energy. An exothermic reaction is neither a necessary nor a sufficient condition for a reaction to be spontaneous.

Answers to Pre-Lab Questions *(Student answers will vary.)*

1. Use the "surface model" described in the *Background* to predict how changing each of the following variables will change how fast a crystalline ionic compound dissolves in water: (a) amount of stirring or agitation; (b) temperature of water; (c) size of the crystals.

    (a) Stirring a solution will help a solute to dissolve faster by increasing the rate at which fresh solvent is brought into contact with the surface of the solute.

Factors Affecting Solution Formation

Teacher's Notes

(b) Increasing the temperature will help a solute to dissolve faster by increasing the average kinetic energy of the solvent molecules and the dissolved ions. The solvent molecules will travel from one region of the solution to another region more quickly as the temperature is raised. This will bring fresh solvent in contact with undissolved solute at a faster rate.

(c) Increasing the size of the solute crystals will decrease the rate at which the solute dissolves in water. As the relative size of the solute crystals increases, their surface area/mass ratio decreases. Decreasing the amount of solute surfaces exposed to the solvent will slow down the rate at which solvent molecules interact with surface ions.

2. Outline a series of tests to determine how each variable will affect the rate at which copper(II) sulfate pentahydrate dissolves in water. Each test should look at the effect of changing only one variable at a time—all of the other variables must be controlled or held constant for comparison.

   There are three independent variables. The dependent variable in each case is the time needed for the solute to dissolve. There are also two variables that must be controlled—the mass of copper sulfate and the volume of water. For each independent variable, test at least three different "settings" or values, one of which may be considered to be a control for that variable. For example, in order to test the effect of temperature as the independent variable, consider room temperature as the control and measure the rate of dissolving at two additional temperatures, one below room temperature and one above room temperature. To test the degree of mixing as the independent variable, vary the number of times the solution is inverted or swirled. It is possible to design the tests in such a way that a single solution will serve as the control for each independent variable to be tested. **Note to teachers:** *One possible scenario is outlined below. It is not practical to use "no mixing" as the control. See the* Lab Hints *section for more information.*

Control:	*Room temperature, constant mixing, fine crystal grade.*
Series A (temperature):	*Ice-cold water, constant mixing, fine crystal grade*
	Hot water, constant mixing, fine crystal grade
Series B (mixing):	*Room temperature, no mixing, fine crystal grade*
	Room temperature, intermittent mixing, fine crystal grade
Series C (crystal size):	*Room temperature, constant mixing, powder*
	Room temperature, constant mixing, medium or large crystals

3. Read the *Materials* section and the recommended *Safety Precautions*. Write a step-by-step procedure for the experiment, including any safety precautions that must be followed. *Note:* There are two crystal sizes of copper sulfate. Use about 0.2 g of the fine crystal grade as the control variable. Fill the test tubes about one-third full with distilled or deionized water.

   See the Supplementary Information *section.*

Teacher Notes

Many students may need help expressing these ideas in the jargon of the discipline, that is, using technical terms. It may help, as noted before, to have students draw conceptual models. The teacher can then introduce the technical terms to express the ideas contained in the pictures.

Flinn ChemTopic™ Labs — Solubility and Solutions

Teacher's Notes

Teacher Notes

Sample Data

Student data will vary.

Data Table*

Test Tube	Temperature	Extent of Mixing	Particle Size	Time to Dissolve	Observations
1	22 °C	Constant	Fine crystals	45 sec	Control solution. Homogeneous, pale blue liquid (no solid).
Effect of Mixing					
2	22 °C	None	Fine crystals	>5 minutes	Undissolved solid; colorless liquid (very faint blue on surface of solid).
3	22 °C	Intermittent	Fine crystals	1 min and 30 sec	Homogeneous, pale blue liquid (no solid).
Effect of Temperature					
4	2 °C	Constant	Fine crystals	1 min and 30 sec	Homogeneous, pale blue liquid (no solid).
5	81 °C	Constant	Fine crystals	20 sec	Homogeneous, pale blue liquid (no solid).
Effect of Particle Size					
6	22 °C	Constant	Powder	32 sec	Homogeneous, pale blue liquid (no solid).
7	22 °C	Constant	Medium crystal	3 min and 40 sec	Homogeneous, pale blue liquid (no solid).

*These are optimum test results. Expect more ambiguous results if students do not choose constant mixing as the control for this variable.

Answers to Post-Lab Questions *(Student answers will vary.)*

1. What effect did mixing or shaking have on the rate at which the solute dissolved in water? Give specific evidence from your tests and explain in terms of the "surface model" for solution formation.

    Mixing or shaking increased the rate at which the solute dissolved in water—minimal dissolving occurred if the mixture was not stirred. The rate of dissolving was also slower when the mixing was intermittent rather than constant. Mixing appears to be a critical variable, which makes sense if fresh solvent must make contact with the surface of the solid in order for the solute to dissolve. **Note to teachers:** *Solution formation is reversible. When the rate of dissolving is equal to the rate of recrystallizing, the solution becomes saturated. If the mixture is not stirred, the solution immediately surrounding the solute quickly becomes saturated.*

*Dissolving is extremely slow if the mixture is not **stirred** in some way. In test tube 2, minimal dissolving was observed even after 30 minutes.*

Factors Affecting Solution Formation

Teacher's Notes

2. How did increasing the temperature of the solvent change the rate at which copper sulfate dissolved in water? Was the opposite effect observed when copper sulfate was dissolved in cold water?

   Increasing the temperature of the water from room temperature to 80 °C doubled the rate at which the solid dissolved (the solid dissolved in half the time). The opposite effect was observed using cold water—the rate at which the solid dissolved was cut in half (it took twice as long to dissolve the solid at 2 °C compared to 22 °C.)

3. Use the definition of temperature and the kinetic theory to explain the effect of temperature on the rate of solution formation for copper sulfate.

   Increasing the temperature increases the average kinetic energy of the solvent molecules (they move faster). As solvent molecules move faster, fresh solvent molecules interact more frequently with the surface of the solid.

4. In some cases, increasing the temperature may be a disadvantage in preparing a solution. Suggest a possible case where heating the solution might be a problem.

   Increasing the temperature of the solution could be a problem if the solute decomposes at higher temperatures. Carbonates, for example, lose carbon dioxide upon heating. **Note to teachers:** *For many ionic solutes, their solubility increases with increasing temperature because their heats of solution are positive. For solutes that have negative heats of solution, their solubility may decrease as the temperature is increased. We would not expect students to know this at this point.*

5. What was the effect of crystal size on the rate of dissolving? How do these results support the surface model for solution formation.

   Increasing the size of the solute crystals (by using a medium-sized crystal lump) decreased the rate at which the solute dissolved. Decreasing the size of the solute crystals (by grinding the crystals to a powder) increased the rate at which the solute dissolved. These results support the surface model for solution formation if we relate crystal size to changes in surface area. Increasing the size of the crystals decreases their overall surface area and thus decreases the amount of surface that is exposed to the solvent molecules. Decreasing the crystal size increases their overall surface area.

Teacher Notes

The effect of temperature on solubility depends on the "differential heat of solution" at saturation. This is not the same as the heat of solution that might be measured in a typical calorimetry experiment.

Teacher's Notes

Teacher Notes

6. Use the results of this experiment to predict how the rate of dissolving would be affected if you tried to dissolve more copper sulfate in a solution that already contained some copper sulfate rather than in distilled water. *Note:* Assume that the total (combined) amount of solute is less than the solubility limit of copper sulfate.

   The results of the mixing experiments suggest that bringing fresh solvent into contact with the solute crystals is a critical variable in the rate of dissolving. It would probably take longer for more copper sulfate to dissolve in the solution than in distilled water. The solubility of a substance determines how much of that solute can dissolve in a given volume of water at a given temperature. Imagine that the water has a specific number of seats in which dissolved solute particles can sit. As these seats become filled, it is harder for an undissolved solute particle to find an empty seat, and it takes that particle longer to find an empty seat before it will dissolve. **Note to teachers:** *Once again, this analogy ignores the fact that solution formation is reversible. If you are introducing solution formation and solubility in terms of equilibrium, then this is a good opportunity to compare the rate of dissolving versus the rate of recrystallizing.*

7. Write a short paragraph describing an optimum procedure for preparing a solution.

   Mixing or stirring appears to be the most important factor governing how fast a solution will form. An optimum procedure for dissolving a substance would always involve stirring the solid to dissolve it in the solvent. If a substance is hard to dissolve even with stirring, several additional measures can be taken to increase the rate at which the solid dissolves. Grinding a solid to obtain a powder will help the solid dissolve faster. If the solid is stable at higher temperatures, then increasing the temperature will also usually increase the rate at which the solid dissolves.

Factors Affecting Solution Formation

Teacher's Notes

Supplementary Information

Sample Procedure

1. Fill a small beaker about one-third full with water. Add several ice cubes and allow the ice water to cool to about 5 °C for use in step 14.

2. Fill a small beaker about half-full with water. Warm on a hot plate to about 80 °C for use in step 17.

3. Using weighing paper or dishes, weigh out five 0.2-g samples of copper sulfate pentahydrate (fine crystals). *Note:* The masses do not have to be exactly identical. Try to keep the masses within the 0.18–0.22 g range.

4. Label three clean test tubes #1–3 and add one 0.2-g sample of copper sulfate to each test tube.

Control Solution

5. Obtain 10 mL of distilled water in a graduated cylinder and measure and record its temperature.

6. Add the room-temperature water to test tube #1. Note the time and swirl, shake or invert the solution at a constant rate (e.g., "flick" the test tube every second).

7. Record the time needed for the solid to dissolve completely.

Effect of Mixing

8. Fill test tube #2 to the same level as test tube #1 with distilled or deionized water. Note the time at which the water was added and place the test tube in a test tube rack. Do not shake or swirl the solution.

9. Record the time needed for the solid to dissolve completely. *Note:* Continue with steps 10–12, but check the solution periodically to see when the solid has dissolved. If the solid has not dissolved after 5 minutes, record this fact along with the solution appearance.

10. Fill test tube #3 to the same level with distilled or deionized water. Note the time and swirl, shake or invert the solution at an intermittent rate (e.g., "flick" the test tube every other second). *Caution:* Do not invert the test tubes unless they are tightly stoppered! Avoid contact of all chemicals with skin and eyes.

11. Record the time needed for the solid to dissolve completely.

12. Empty the contents of test tubes #2 and 3 as directed by your instructor. Rinse the test tubes twice with distilled water and relabel them #4 and 5.

Effect of Temperature

13. Add one 0.2-g sample of copper sulfate from step 3 to each test tube #4 and 5.

14. Measure and record the temperature of ice-cold water in the beaker from step 1.

Teacher Notes

This is an ideal procedure—most students will not think several steps ahead, as recommended in steps 1–4. Use the sample procedure as an alternative student handout, if desired.

Flinn ChemTopic™ Labs — Solubility and Solutions

Teacher's Notes

Teacher Notes

15. Add 10 mL of the ice-cold water to test tube #4. Note the time and swirl, shake or invert the solution at a constant rate (e.g., "flick" the test tube every second).

16. Record the time needed for the solid to dissolve completely. *Note:* Continue with steps 17–20, but check the solution periodically to see when the solid has dissolved. If the solid has not dissolved after 5 minutes, record this fact along with the solution appearance.

17. Measure and record the temperature of hot water in the beaker from step 2.

18. Add 10 mL of the hot water to test tube #5. Note the time and swirl, shake, or invert the solution at a constant rate (e.g., "flick" the test tube every second).

19. Record the time needed for the solid to dissolve completely.

20. Empty the contents of test tubes #4 and 5 as directed by your instructor. Rinse the test tubes twice with distilled water and relabel them #6 and 7.

Effect of Particle Size

21. Obtain a medium sized crystal (the size of a pea) of copper sulfate and measure and record its mass. Try to use a crystal that is about 0.2 g in mass.

22. Add the copper sulfate crystal to test tube #6, followed by 10 mL of distilled water. Note the time and swirl, shake, or invert the solution at a constant rate (e.g., "flick" the test tube every second).

23. Record the time needed for the solid to dissolve completely. Continue with steps 24–27, but check the solution periodically to see when the solid has dissolved. If the solid has not dissolved after 5 minutes, record this fact along with the solution appearance.

24. Grind some copper sulfate fine crystals in a mortar and pestle to obtain a fine powder. Using weighing paper, weigh out a 0.2-g sample of powder.

25. Add the copper sulfate fine powder to test tube #7, followed by 10 mL of distilled water. Note the time and swirl, shake, or invert the solution at a constant rate (e.g., "flick" the test tube every second).

26. Record the time needed for the powder to dissolve completely.

27. Empty the contents of test tubes #6 and 7 as directed by your instructor. Wash and rinse the test tubes.

Teacher's Notes

Factors Affecting Solution Formation Data Table

Test Tube	Temperature	Extent of Mixing	Particle Size	Time to Dissolve	Observations
1					Control sample.
Effect of Mixing					
2					
3					
Effect of Temperature					
4					
5					
Effect of Particle Size					
6					
7					

Teacher Notes

Use this sample data table as an alternative student handout, if desired.

Teacher Notes

It's in Their Nature
Solute–Solvent Interactions

Introduction

"Oil and water do not mix." How many times have you heard this old saying? As metaphor, it is often used to explain why relationships between opposites are difficult or even impossible. Let's trace this metaphor back to its source—the nature of oil and water, solutes and solvents, and why some substances do not dissolve in or mix well with others.

Concepts

- Solute and solvent
- Polar vs. nonpolar
- Intermolecular forces
- Miscibility of liquids

Background

A solution is a homogeneous mixture of two or more substances. The word homogeneous means that a solution must be uniform throughout its contents. The composition or concentration of a solution can be changed by changing the amount of the solute (the minor component) dissolved in a given amount of the solvent (the major component). Although many common solutions contain solids dissolved in liquids, both the solute and the solvent may exist in any phase (solid, liquid or gas). Solubility is a characteristic property of a pure substance and can be used to help identify different substances. Thus, a chemistry handbook will usually report the solubility of a substance in different solvents along with other physical properties such as melting point, density, etc.

When a solute dissolves in a solvent, the attractive forces acting between solute particles and those between solvent molecules must be broken and replaced by new attractive forces between the solute and solvent. The nature and strength of the attractive forces among solute and solvent particles influences whether a solute will dissolve in a solvent. Many ionic compounds, for example, dissolve readily in water. Water is a highly polar molecule, with a great degree of charge separation between the oxygen and hydrogen atoms in its O—H bonds. Upon dissolving in water, an ionic compound breaks apart into its component ions, which are attracted to the partially charged ends of the highly polar water molecules.

Molecular compounds consist of molecules—groups of atoms held together by covalent bonds—rather than ions. The physical properties of a molecular compound, including its solubility, depend on the polarity of the molecules. Molecules are classified as polar or nonpolar based on the nature of the electron sharing among the atoms in a molecule. Polar molecules tend to exert stronger attractive forces than nonpolar molecules. The polarity of a compound determines the types of intermolecular attractive forces between molecules and is an important factor influencing the solubility of solutes and solvents.

Refer to your textbook for a thorough explanation of solute–solvent interactions and the enthalpy and entropy of solution formation in water. There are many misconceptions about the nature of the "hydrophobic" effect (and the name itself may do more harm than good).

It's in Their Nature – Page 2

Teacher Notes

Experiment Overview

The purpose of this experiment is to investigate the solubility of ionic, polar, and nonpolar compounds in a variety of solvents. The solubility patterns of different solutes and solvents will be used to classify compounds and to understand the nature of the interactions between solute and solvent particles.

Pre-Lab Questions

1. Is the iodine molecule polar or nonpolar? Explain.

2. The formula of hexane is CH_3—CH_2—CH_2—CH_2—CH_2—CH_3. Based on its structural formula, is hexane a polar or nonpolar compound? Explain.

3. Draw the structure of a water molecule and explain why it is polar. Show by means of a diagram the types of attractive forces acting between water molecules and also between water molecules and dissolved ions such as Na^+ and Cl^- ions.

Materials

Benzoic acid, C_6H_5COOH, 0.5 g
Cholesterol, $C_{27}H_{46}O$, 0.5 g
Dextrose, $C_6H_{12}O_6$, 0.5 g
Ethyl alcohol, C_2H_5OH, 15 mL
Hexane, C_6H_{14}, 17 mL
Iodine, I_2, 0.5 g
Potassium nitrate, KNO_3, 0.5 g
Toluene, $C_6H_5CH_3$, 6 mL

Beral-type pipets, 4
Distilled or deionized water
Graduated cylinder, 10-mL
Paper towels
Spatula
Test tubes, 6
Test tube rack
Wash bottle

Safety Precautions

Ethyl alcohol, hexane, and toluene are flammable organic solvents and dangerous fire risks. Keep away from flames and other sources of ignition. Addition of denaturant makes ethyl alcohol poisonous. Toluene is moderately toxic by ingestion, inhalation, and skin absorption. Work with these solvents in a well-ventilated lab only and avoid breathing their vapors. Iodine is toxic by ingestion or inhalation. It is a skin and eye irritant and will stain skin and clothing. Avoid contact of all chemicals with eyes and skin. Wear chemical splash goggles and chemical-resistant gloves and apron. Wash hands thoroughly with soap and water before leaving the lab.

Page 3 – **It's in Their Nature**

Teacher Notes

Procedure

Part A. Solubility of Iodine

1. Obtain four clean test tubes and place them in a test tube rack. Using Table 1 as a guide, add about 2 mL of the appropriate solvent to each test tube. *Note:* Use a graduated cylinder to measure and add 2 mL of water to test tube #1, then compare liquid levels to add about the same volume of other solvents to test tubes #2–4.

Table 1.

Test tube	1	2	3	4
Solvent	Water	Ethyl alcohol	Hexane	Toluene

2. Using a spatula, add one crystal of iodine to each test tube.

3. Gently swirl or tap each test tube and observe the mixtures. Beneath the name of each solvent in the data table, record whether iodine is soluble or insoluble in the solvent and the color of the solution (if appropriate).

4. Dispose of the contents of the test tubes in the "Iodine Waste" container provided by your instructor.

5. Rinse each test tube twice with water and dry them with a paper towel for use in Part B.

Part B. Miscibility of Solvents

6. Place six clean test tubes in a test tube rack. Add about 2 mL (40 drops) of water to test tubes #1, 2, and 3.

7. Add about 2 mL of hexane to test tubes #4 and 5.

8. Add about 2 mL of toluene to test tube #6.

9. Using Table 2 as a guide, add 20 drops (about 1 mL) of a second solvent to each test tube.

Table 2.

Test tube	1	2	3	4	5	6
First solvent (2 mL)	Water	Water	Water	Hexane	Hexane	Toluene
Second solvent (1 mL)	Ethyl alcohol	Hexane	Toluene	Ethyl alcohol	Toluene	Ethyl alcohol

10. Gently swirl or tap each test tube to mix the contents.

11. Next to the name of each solvent pair in the data table, record whether the two liquids form one or two layers upon standing. If the mixtures separate into two layers, report which solvent is the upper layer.

For convenience, have students mark the 2-mL level on each test tube.

It's in Their Nature – Page 4

12. Dispose of the contents of the test tubes in the "Organic Waste" container provided by your instructor. Rinse each test tube twice with water and dry them with a paper towel before using them in Part C.

Part C. Solutes and Solvents

13. Obtain six clean test tubes and label them #1–6.

14. Add about 2 mL (40 drops) of the appropriate solvent to each test tube, as shown in Table 3.

Table 3.

Test tube	1	2	3	4	5	6
Solvent	Water	Ethyl alcohol	Hexane	Water	Ethyl alcohol	Hexane

15. Using a clean spatula, add a small amount (about the size of a grain of rice) of dextrose to test tubes #1, 2, and 3.

16. Wipe the spatula with a clean paper towel, then add a small amount (about the size of a grain of rice) of potassium nitrate to test tubes #4, 5, and 6.

17. Gently swirl or tap each test tube to mix the contents.

18. In the data table, record whether each substance is soluble or insoluble in each solvent.

19. Dispose of the test tube contents as directed by your instructor.

20. Rinse each test tube once with about 1 mL of the appropriate solvent, and then add about 2 mL of fresh solvent to each tube. Use the same solvent arrangement shown in Table 3.

21. Using a clean spatula, add a small amount (about the size of a grain of rice) of cholesterol to test tubes #1, 2, and 3.

22. Wipe the spatula with a clean paper towel, then add a small amount (about the size of a grain of rice) of benzoic acid to test tubes #4, 5, and 6.

23. Gently swirl or tap each test tube to mix the contents.

24. In the data table, record whether each substance is soluble or insoluble in each solvent.

25. Dispose of the test tube contents as directed by your instructor. Wash and rinse the test tubes.

Teacher Notes

Students should not be too impatient in judging the solubility of compounds in Part C. It may be necessary to swirl each test tube a few minutes in order to observe the solubility trends.

Teacher Notes

Name: _____

Class/Lab Period: _____

It's in Their Nature

Data Tables

Part A. Solubility of Iodine

Solvent (Test Tube)			
Water (1)	Ethyl alcohol (2)	Hexane (3)	Toluene (4)

Part B. Miscibility of Solvents

Solvent Pair (Test Tube)		Solvent Pair (Test Tube)	
Water Ethyl alcohol (1)		Hexane Ethyl alcohol (4)	
Water Hexane (2)		Hexane Toluene (5)	
Water Toluene (3)		Toluene Ethyl alcohol (6)	

Part C. Solutes and Solvents

	Water	Ethyl alcohol	Hexane
Dextrose			
Potassium nitrate			
Cholesterol			
Benzoic acid			

It's in Their Nature – Page 6

Post-Lab Questions *(Use a separate sheet of paper to answer the following questions.)*

1. In which solvents is iodine soluble? In which solvents is iodine insoluble?

2. Define the term miscibility, then circle the correct choice in each statement to summarize the miscibility of the solvent pairs tested in Part B:

   Water and ethyl alcohol are *(miscible/immiscible)*.
   Water and hexane are *(miscible/immiscible)*.
   Water and toluene are *(miscible/immiscible)*.
   Hexane and ethyl alcohol are *(miscible/immiscible)*.
   Hexane and toluene are *(miscible/immiscible)*.
   Toluene and ethyl alcohol are *(miscible/immiscible)*.

3. Rank the four solvents tested in Parts A and B in order from most polar to least polar (nonpolar). Which two solvents are most alike in their polarity? Explain your reasoning.

4. Write a general statement describing the solubility of nonpolar solutes in different solvents and suggest a reason for this pattern.

5. Potassium nitrate (Part C) is an ionic compound. Write a general statement describing the solubility of ionic compounds in different solvents.

6. Dextrose, cholesterol, and benzoic acid are molecular (organic) compounds. Based on their solubility patterns in Part C, arrange these three solutes in order from most polar to least polar. Explain your reasoning.

7. Based on its solubility, would you expect cholesterol to be soluble in the bloodstream? Where does cholesterol tend to accumulate in the body? Why?

8. Vitamins are classified as either water-soluble or fat-soluble. The structures of Vitamin C (water-soluble) and Vitamin A (fat-soluble) are shown below. Identify the features of these molecules that give them their characteristic solubility.

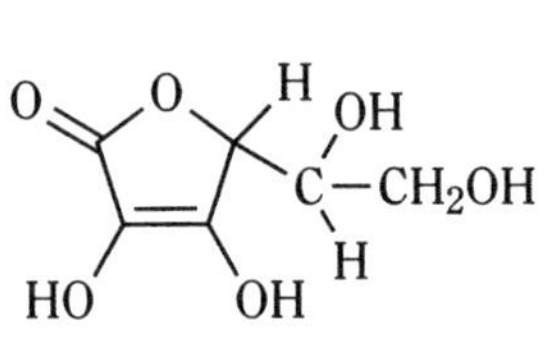

   Vitamin C 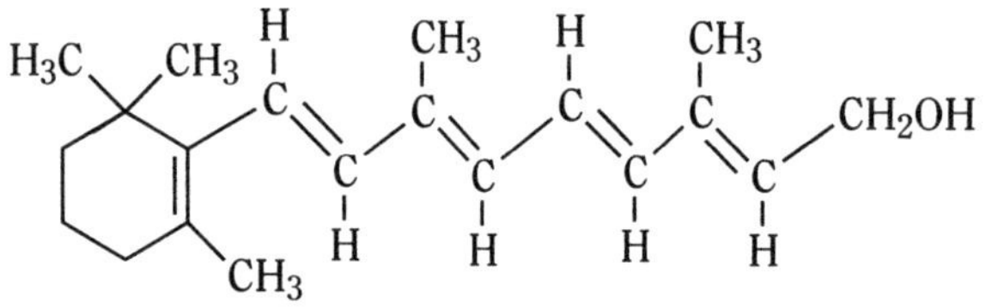   Vitamin A

9. The simple rule *"Like dissolves like"* is often used to describe the solubility of a substance in different solvents. Write a short paragraph discussing your evidence for this rule. Include in your discussion where you think this rule works best and where it seems to be less reliable. Give specific examples to back up your statements.

10. *(Optional)* A drop of motor oil spilled on wet pavement will quickly spread out into a thin film. A drop of water spilled on a greasy plate, however, will bead up into a little sphere. Use these observations, and the nature of solute–solvent interactions, to explain why oil and water do not mix.

Teacher Notes

Teacher's Notes
It's in Their Nature

Master Materials List *(for a class of 30 students working in groups of four)*

Benzoic acid, C_6H_5COOH, 8 g	Beral-type pipets, 60
Cholesterol, $C_{27}H_{46}O$, 8 g	Distilled or deionized water
Dextrose, $C_6H_{12}O_6$, 8 g	Graduated cylinders, 10-mL, 15
Ethyl alcohol, C_2H_5OH, 225 mL	Paper towels
Hexane, C_6H_{14}, 255 mL	Spatulas, 15
Iodine, I_2, 8 g	Test tubes, 13 × 100 mm, 90
Potassium nitrate, KNO_3, 8 g	Test tube racks, 15
Toluene, $C_6H_5CH_3$, 100 mL	Wash bottles, 15

Safety Precautions

Ethyl alcohol, hexane, and toluene are flammable organic solvents and dangerous fire risks. Keep away from flames and other sources of ignition. Addition of denaturant makes ethyl alcohol poisonous. Toluene is moderately toxic by ingestion, inhalation, and skin absorption. Work with these solvents in a well-ventilated lab only and avoid breathing their vapors. Iodine is toxic by ingestion or inhalation. It is a skin and eye irritant and will stain skin and clothing. Avoid contact of all chemicals with eyes and skin. Wear chemical splash goggles and chemical-resistant gloves and apron. Remind students to wash their hands thoroughly with soap and water before leaving the lab. Please consult current Material Safety Data Sheets for additional safety, handling, and disposal information.

Disposal

Consult your current *Flinn Scientific Catalog/Reference Manual* for general guidelines and specific procedures governing the disposal of laboratory waste. Waste solutions containing iodine (Part A) may be disposed of by reduction with sodium thiosulfate according to Flinn Suggested Disposal Method #12. Waste solutions containing volatile organic solvents may be disposed of according to Flinn Suggested Disposal Method #18a.

Lab Hints

- The laboratory work for this experiment can reasonably be completed in one 50-minute lab period. To cut down on the amount of aqueous organic waste generated using organic solvents, consider assigning this experiment as a collaborative classroom activity with different groups doing Parts A, B, and C individually and then sharing their results with each other.

- For best results, set up an "Iodine Waste" container and an "Organic Waste" container in central locations in the lab (the hood is ideal) for immediate collection of waste solutions. Add aqueous sodium thiosulfate solution (50%) to the iodine waste container beforehand and the solution will be ready to dispose of down the drain with plenty of excess water when the lab is done.

- The recommended solvents are "hexanes," a mixture of n-hexane and other isomers, and 95% denatured ethyl alcohol.

Potassium nitrate carries a warning—"strong oxidant, fire and explosion risk when heated or in contact with organic materials." The warning is serious, but the microscale amount of potassium nitrate (equivalent to a grain of rice) used in this experiment is small enough to avoid this hazard. Do not allow any flames, heating or ignition anywhere in the lab during this activity. Do not scale the experiment up.

Teacher's Notes

- The solutes and solvents for this lab were selected to give an interesting range of results. This list is not cast in stone, however—many common chemicals may be substituted for the ones used in this experiment. Isopropyl alcohol, for example, will give similar results to ethyl alcohol. Sucrose may also be substituted for dextrose. Any simple ionic compound may be used in place of potassium nitrate. Heptane or mineral oil are good substitutes for hexane. Look around your stockroom and choose compounds that will give similar solubility patterns as the materials listed in the *Sample Data* section.

Teaching Tip

- Organic chemistry is an interesting and important part of chemistry education, even at the high school level. Don't wait until the end of the year to introduce some organic chemistry into the curriculum—you won't have time! Let the organic chemistry come naturally, as it does in this experiment, by using organic chemicals as examples to teach the principles of general chemistry. Use this lab as a springboard to highlight and discuss the applications of organic compounds in our daily lives.

Answers to Pre-Lab Questions *(Student answers will vary.)*

1. Is the iodine molecule polar or nonpolar? Explain.

   The two iodine atoms in the iodine molecule share electrons equally in the covalent bond joining them. Because the electrons are equally shared between the two atoms, the bond and the molecule itself are nonpolar.

2. The formula of hexane is $CH_3-CH_2-CH_2-CH_2-CH_2-CH_3$. Based on its structural formula, is hexane a polar or nonpolar compound? Explain.

   Hexane is a hydrocarbon molecule consisting of only C—H and C—C bonds. Because carbon and hydrogen atoms have similar electronegativity values, the covalent bonds between these atoms have equally shared electrons. The molecule is nonpolar.

3. Draw the structure of a water molecule and explain why it is polar. Show by means of a diagram the types of attractive forces acting between water molecules and also between water molecules and dissolved ions such as Na⁺ and Cl⁻ ions.

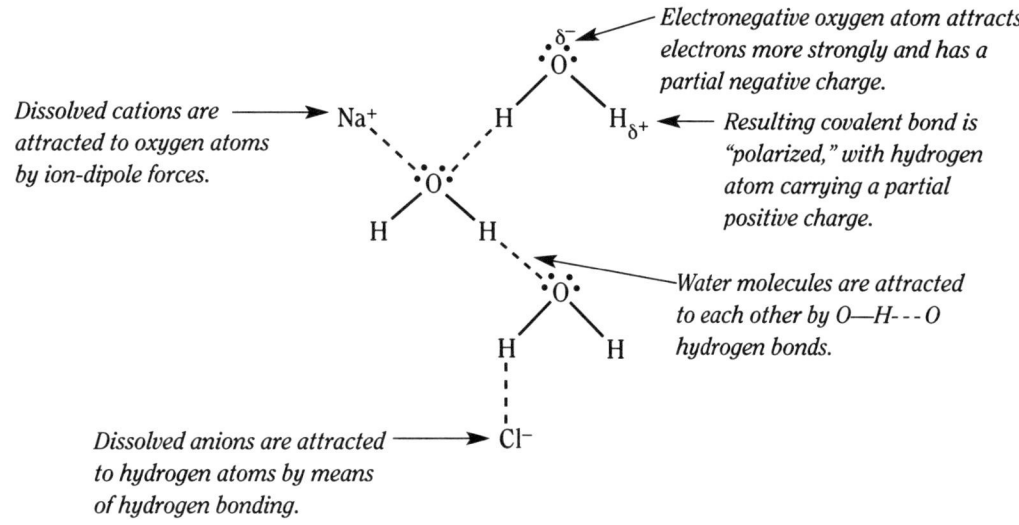

Flinn ChemTopic™ Labs — Solubility and Solutions

Teacher Notes

Sample Data

Student data will vary.

Data Tables

Part A. Solubility of Iodine

Solvent (Test Tube)			
Water (1)	**Ethyl alcohol (2)**	**Hexane (3)**	**Toluene (4)**
Insoluble	Partially soluble (Brown solution)	Soluble (Purple solution)	Soluble (Dark red solution)

Part B. Miscibility of Solvents

Solvent Pair (Test Tube)		Solvent Pair (Test Tube)	
Water Ethyl alcohol (1)	One liquid layer	**Hexane Ethyl alcohol (4)**	One liquid layer
Water Hexane (2)	Two layers (Upper layer—hexane)	**Hexane Toluene (5)**	One liquid layer
Water Toluene (3)	Two layers (Upper layer—toluene)	**Toluene Ethyl alcohol (6)**	One liquid layer

Part C. Solutes and Solvents

	Water	Ethyl alcohol	Hexane
Dextrose	Soluble	Slightly soluble	Insoluble
Potassium nitrate	Soluble	Slightly soluble	Insoluble
Cholesterol	Insoluble	Insoluble	Soluble
Benzoic acid	Slightly soluble	Soluble	Insoluble

Notice that iodine forms different color solutions in different solvents. The beautiful red color of iodine in toluene is due to the formation of a classic charge–transfer complex between toluene and iodine.

It's in Their Nature

Teacher's Notes

Answers to Post-Lab Questions *(Student answers will vary.)*

1. In which solvents is iodine soluble? In which solvents is iodine insoluble?

    Iodine is soluble in hexane and toluene, partially or slightly soluble in ethyl alcohol, and insoluble in water.

2. Define the term miscibility, then circle the correct choice in each statement to summarize the miscibility of the solvent pairs tested in Part B:

    Miscibility is the term used to describe the mutual solubility of liquids in one another. Two liquids are said to be miscible if they dissolve freely in each other in all proportions to form a single liquid phase when mixed.

    Water and ethyl alcohol are *(**miscible**/immiscible)*.
    Water and hexane are *(miscible/**immiscible**)*.
    Water and toluene are *(miscible/**immiscible**)*.
    Hexane and ethyl alcohol are *(**miscible**/immiscible)*.
    Hexane and toluene are *(**miscible**/immiscible)*.
    Toluene and ethyl alcohol are *(**miscible**/immiscible)*.

3. Rank the four solvents tested in Parts A and B in order from most polar to least polar (nonpolar). Which two solvents are most alike in their polarity? Explain your reasoning.

    From most polar to nonpolar: Water > ethyl alcohol > hexane and toluene. Ethyl alcohol is intermediate in polarity between water (which is highly polar) and hexane or toluene (which are nonpolar). Thus, ethyl alcohol is miscible with all of the solvents tested. Hexane and toluene are most alike in their polarity—they are miscible with each other, and both are immiscible with water.

4. Write a general statement describing the solubility of nonpolar solutes in different solvents and suggest a reason for this pattern.

    Nonpolar solutes dissolve in nonpolar solvents but do not dissolve in water, a highly polar solvent. The solubility of nonpolar solutes in other polar solvents varies—they may be partially soluble. Nonpolar solutes and solvents have similar attractive forces.

5. Potassium nitrate (Part C) is an ionic compound. Write a general statement describing the solubility of ionic compounds in different solvents.

    Ionic compounds dissolve in water, a highly polar solvent. They do not dissolve at all in nonpolar solvents.

Teacher Notes

6. Dextrose, cholesterol, and benzoic acid are molecular (organic) compounds. Based on their solubility patterns in Part C, arrange these three solutes in order from most polar to least polar. Explain your reasoning.

   From most polar to least polar: Dextrose > benzoic acid > cholesterol. The fact that dextrose is soluble only in water and only slightly in ethyl alcohol suggests that it is a highly polar compound (its solubility pattern is the same as that of potassium nitrate, an ionic compound). Cholesterol is soluble only in hexane, a nonpolar solvent, and is thus a nonpolar compound. Benzoic acid is slightly soluble in water, soluble in ethyl alcohol, and insoluble in hexane, suggesting that it is intermediate in polarity. **Note to teachers:** *Benzoic acid is soluble in hot water.*

7. Based on its solubility, would you expect cholesterol to be soluble in the bloodstream? Where does cholesterol tend to accumulate in the body? Why?

   Cholesterol is insoluble in the bloodstream. It tends to accumulate in fatty tissues and, of course, in the walls (nonpolar membranes) of blood vessels. **Note to teachers:** *How then does cholesterol get carried through the bloodstream? That's the role of the lipoproteins (both the bad LDL and the good HDL) that are so much in the news. (Many adults can quote their LDL/HDL ratios the way sports fans can quote the batting averages of their favorite baseball players.) Lipoproteins act as emulsifying agents, carrying cholesterol through the bloodstream.*

8. Vitamins are classified as either water-soluble or fat-soluble. The structures of Vitamin C (water-soluble) and Vitamin A (fat-soluble) are shown below. Identify the features of these molecules that give them their characteristic solubility.

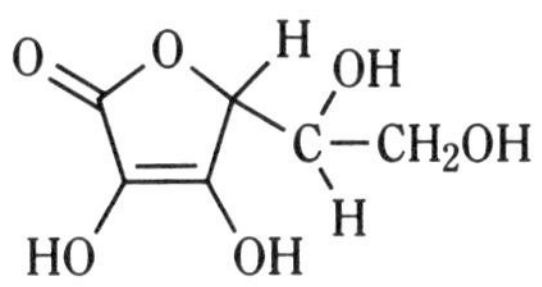

   Vitamin C

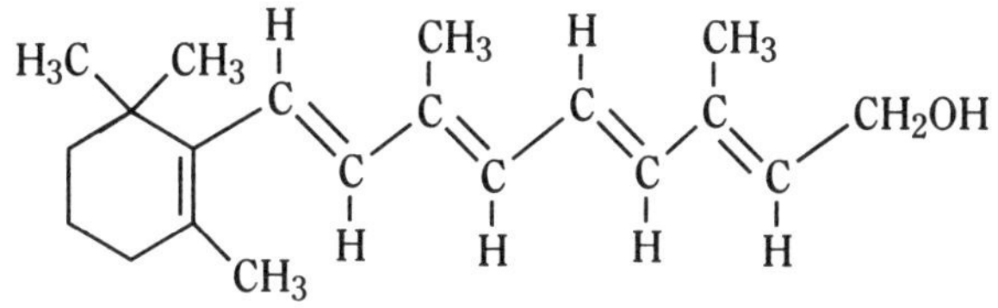

   Vitamin A

   Vitamin C contains many polar C—O and O—H bonds. It is a highly polar compound and is thus soluble in water and other polar solvents. Vitamin A consists almost entirely of nonpolar C—H, C—C, and C═C bonds and is a nonpolar compound. It does not dissolve in water, but does dissolve in fatty tissue, which contains nonpolar fats and oils.

Teacher's Notes

9. The simple rule *"Like dissolves like"* is often used to describe the solubility of a substance in different solvents. Write a short paragraph discussing your evidence for this rule. Include in your discussion where you think this rule works best and where it seems to be less reliable. Give specific examples to back up your statements.

    The rule "like dissolves like" seems to work best at the two extremes. Thus, nonpolar solutes tend to dissolve only in nonpolar solvents (cholesterol in hexane, iodine in hexane or toluene). Similarly, ionic and very highly polar compounds (potassium nitrate and dextrose) dissolve only in water, a highly polar solvent. Compounds of intermediate polarity exhibit both tendencies. Thus, ethyl alcohol is miscible with both water and hexane.

10. *(Optional)* A drop of motor oil spilled on wet pavement will quickly spread out into a thin film. A drop of water spilled on a greasy plate, however, will bead up into a little sphere. Use these observations, and the nature of solute–solvent interactions, to explain why oil and water do not mix.

    Note to teachers: *There are many misconceptions about why oil and water do not mix. In biology classes, students may learn about the "hydrophobic" effect, which suggests that oil and water molecules somehow repel one another. The fact that oil will spread out into a thin film on wet pavement belies this notion—clearly oil molecules are attracted to surface water molecules, at the very least. In looking at solubility, there are four factors to be considered: the energy required to disrupt attractive forces among solute molecules, the energy required to disrupt attractive forces among solvent molecules, the energy released due to attractive forces between solute and solvent molecules, and the entropy of mixing. Oil and water do not mix because of the second energy term. Water molecules are much more attracted to other water molecules than to oil molecules. The evidence for this is the way water beads up on a sheet of wax paper.*

Page 1 – **Solubility and Temperature**

Teacher Notes

Solubility and Temperature
A Solubility Curve

Introduction

Solubility, defined as the amount of solute that will dissolve in a given amount of solvent, depends on temperature. The solubility of potassium nitrate, for example, increases from 14 g in 100 g of water at 0 °C to about 247 g in 100 g of water at 100 °C—a 1700% increase! While these solubility facts are interesting, they do not allow us to predict the solubility of potassium nitrate at any other temperature. The temperature dependence for the solubility of a substance can only be determined by experiment, by constructing a solubility curve.

Concepts

- Solubility
- Saturated solution
- Saturation temperature
- Solubility curve

Background

A solution that contains the maximum amount of solute that will dissolve at a particular temperature is called a saturated solution. The only practical way to know for sure that a solution is saturated is whether or not there is undissolved solid present. Undissolved solute plays an active role in the saturated solution. For an ionic compound, ions continually break apart from the undissolved crystal and enter the solution. At the same time, dissolved ions from the solution also recombine to form new crystals. When the solution is saturated, the rate at which the solid dissolves is exactly equal to the rate at which solid recrystalizes from the solution. As a result, the mass of dissolved solute in solution remains constant once the solution is saturated—as long as the temperature does not change. Since the solubility of a substance depends on temperature, the amount of dissolved solute present in a saturated solution also depends on temperature. The solubility of a solute is usually reported as the mass of solute in grams that will dissolve in 100 grams of solvent at a specified temperature. The temperature at which a saturated solution is prepared is called the saturation temperature.

In this experiment we will prepare a series of solutions, each containing a premeasured amount of potassium nitrate in a known amount of water. The mixtures will be heated to 80–90 °C until all the solid has dissolved. The solutions will then be cooled until the first signs of crystal formation are observed. The temperature at which crystals first appear is the saturation temperature for that concentration of potassium nitrate. The solubility curve for potassium nitrate will be generated by graphing the solubility of potassium nitrate versus the saturation temperature for each solution.

Experiment Overview

The purpose of this experiment is to construct a solubility curve for potassium nitrate in water by measuring saturation temperatures for six different solution concentrations. Working in groups of four, each pair of students will prepare three different solutions and measure their corresponding saturation temperatures. The solubility of potassium nitrate in each solution will be calculated and plotted against the saturation temperature to construct the solubility curve for potassium nitrate in water.

Potassium nitrate is the classic solute for solubility curve determinations because of its steep increase in solubility as a function of temperature. Other solutes that may be used include potassium bromide, potassium chloride, ammonium chloride, and potassium chlorate. See the Lab Hints *section for more information.*

Solubility and Temperature – Page 2

Pre-Lab Questions

1. Many solutes, including potassium nitrate, have a tendency to remain in solution even after it has been cooled to below the saturation point. This phenomenon is known as supersaturation. Read the entire *Procedure* section carefully. What measure is taken to prevent supersaturation during this experiment?

2. A mixture containing 2.75 g of ammonium chloride (NH_4Cl) in 5.0 g of water was heated to dissolve the solid and then allowed to cool in air. At 61 °C, the first crystals appeared in solution. What is the solubility of ammonium chloride (in g of NH_4Cl per 100 g of water) at 61 °C?

3. The solubility of ammonium chloride in water was measured as described in this experiment and graphed as follows. Use the solubility curve to predict the solubility of ammonium chloride in water at 40 °C.

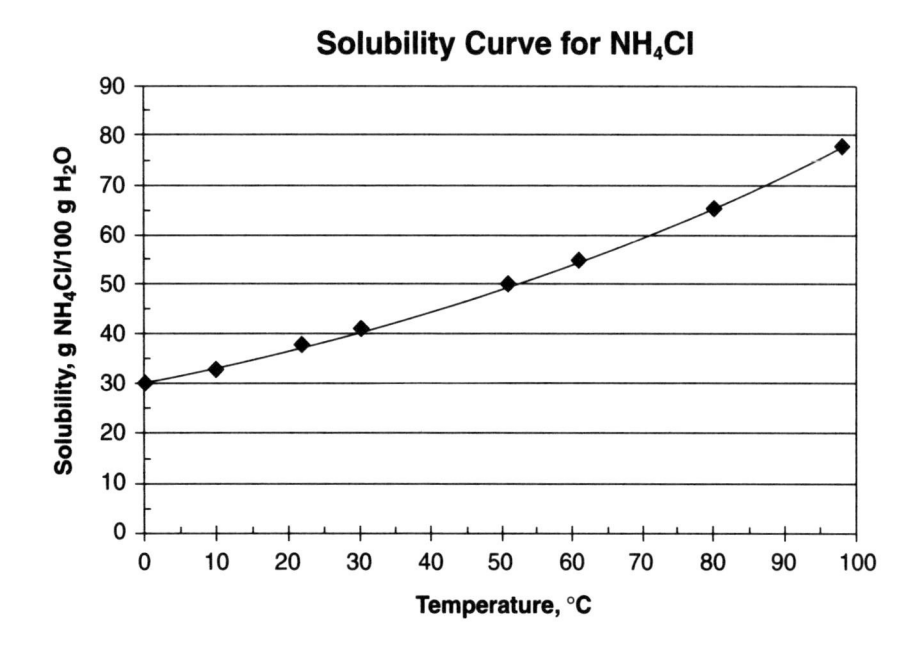

Solubility Curve for NH_4Cl

4. One of the students doing the experiment only had time to measure the saturation temperatures for three solutions at 51 °C, 61 °C, and 80 °C, respectively. Looking at the graph above, do you think the student would have been able to accurately predict the shape of the solubility curve based on these three points? Explain.

Materials

Potassium nitrate, KNO_3, about 3 g
Distilled or deionized water
Balance, centigram precision
Gloves, heat-resistant, or Heat protector
Hot plate
Spatula
Beakers, 50- and 250-mL
Beral-type pipet, thin stem
Test tubes, small, 3
Test tube clamp or holder
Thermometer, digital
Wax pencil or labeling pen

Teacher Notes

The recommended size of test tubes is always specified in the Teacher's Notes *section. This is to avoid having students get too picky if their test tubes are only 12 × 75 mm rather than 13 × 100 mm. Compare the sizes recommended in the* Master Materials List *in the* Teacher's Notes *with your lab equipment and advise students appropriately.*

Page 3 – Solubility and Temperature

Teacher Notes

Safety Precautions

Potassium nitrate in solid form is a strong oxidant and a fire and explosion risk when heated or in contact with organic materials. It is also a skin irritant. Avoid contact with skin and eyes. Wear chemical splash goggles and chemical-resistant gloves and apron. Use caution when working with a hot water bath and a hot plate. Wear heat-resistant gloves or a heat protector when handling hot glassware. Wash hands thoroughly with soap and water before leaving the laboratory.

Procedure

1. Form a working group with three other students and divide into two pairs. Each pair of students will prepare three different solution concentrations (A–C) and measure their saturation temperatures. One pair of students will use the Series I masses shown in the reagents table in step 4, the other pair of students will use the Series II masses. Both pairs of students may share the same hot water bath (step 2).

2. Prepare a hot water bath (80–90 °C) for use in step 10: Fill a 250-mL beaker about two-thirds full with hot tap water and place it on a hot plate at a medium-high setting.

3. Obtain three clean and dry test tubes and label them A, B, and C. Measure and record the mass of each empty test tube in the data table.

4. Using the following table as a guide, add the recommended amount of potassium nitrate to each test tube A–C. Note that the masses given are ranges—anywhere in this mass range is fine, as long the exact mass used in step 5 is recorded.

Test tube	A	B	C
Mass of KNO_3, g (Series I)	0.45–0.50 g	0.70–0.80 g	1.20–1.30 g
Mass of KNO_3, g (Series II)	0.35–0.40 g	0.90–1.00 g	1.50–1.60g

5. Measure and record the combined mass of each test tube and potassium nitrate.

6. Use a clean, thin-stem pipet to add 20 drops of distilled water to each test tube A–C.

7. Place a 50-mL beaker on the balance pan to support the test tubes. Zero (tare) the balance with the empty beaker in place, then place test tube A in the beaker and measure the mass of the test tube and its contents. Record the total mass of the test tube plus solid plus water in the data table. *Note:* The mass of water in each test tube should be at least 0.90 g. If not, add one or two more drops of water to the tube and measure the total mass again.

8. Repeat step 7 for test tubes B and C.

9. Place all of the labeled test tubes in the hot water bath.

10. Immerse the thermometer in test tube C. Gently stir the mixture in test tube C using an up-and-down motion of the thermometer until the solid dissolves completely. *Note:* At this point the solids in the other test tubes should also have dissolved, even without stirring, since they contain less solid.

Microscale technique is important in steps 6 and 7. The mass of water must be in the 0.9–1.1 g range to avoid having too concentrated or too dilute solutions.

27   Solubility and Temperature

Solubility and Temperature – Page 4

11. Wearing gloves or using a heat protector, remove the hot water bath from the heat source.

12. Use a test tube clamp to remove test tube C from the hot water bath and allow the tube and contents to cool slowly in air. Observe the solution closely to watch for the first signs of crystallization.

13. Move the thermometer gently up and down to stir the solution, make sure it is homogeneous, and ensure constant, even cooling. Stirring the solution will also encourage crystal formation and prevent supersaturation.

14. Measure and record the temperature the instant crystallization begins in the test tube (this is the saturation temperature). *Note:* The crystals will be colorless in a colorless solution and will not be easy to see. Watch closely—it will look like snow!

15. Remove the thermometer from the test tube and wipe it once with a clean paper towel to remove potassium nitrate crystals. Warm the thermometer briefly in the hot water bath, dry it with a paper towel, and place it in test tube B.

16. Repeat steps 12–15 with test tubes B and A, *in that order*. Remember to record the saturation temperature for each solution in the data table and to clean the thermometer before transferring it to a new solution.

17. Share the data for the Series I and Series II solutions between both pairs of students in your working group. Complete the data table for all solutions (Series I and Series II).

18. Dispose of the potassium nitrate solutions as directed by your instructor.

Teacher Notes

Pairs of students working together will have to coordinate their work in step 11. Do not remove the hot water bath from the heat source until all of the samples (Series I and Series II) have dissolved.

Teacher Notes

Name: _____

Class/Lab Period: _____

Solubility and Temperature

Data Table

Sample		Mass of empty test tube	Mass of test tube plus KNO$_3$	Mass of test tube plus KNO$_3$ plus water	Saturation temperature
Series I	A				
	B				
	C				
Series II	A				
	B				
	C				

Post-Lab Calculations and Analysis

(Use a separate sheet of paper to answer the following questions.)

Construct a *Results Table* to summarize the results of the following calculations for all solutions (Series I and Series II).

1. Calculate the mass of potassium nitrate and the mass of water in each solution.

2. Calculate the ratio of the mass of potassium nitrate to the mass of water for each solution. *Example:* For 0.47 g KNO$_2$ and 1.06 g H$_2$O, the mass ratio is equal to 0.47 g/1.06 g or 0.44.

3. Multiply the mass ratio by 100 to determine the concentration of each saturated solution in grams of potassium nitrate per 100 grams of water.

4. Plot a graph of solubility of potassium nitrate (in g of solute/100 g of water) on the y-axis versus temperature on the x-axis. Scale each axis as necessary. Draw a smooth, best-fit *curved line* though the data points. Don't forget to label each axis and give the graph a title!

5. Using your graph, estimate the solubility of potassium nitrate in water at (a) 0 °C; (b) 50 °C; and (c) 100 °C.

6. Using your graph, predict the temperature at which each of the following mixtures of potassium nitrate in water would form a saturated solution: (a) 25 g KNO$_3$ in 25 g H$_2$O; (b) 100 g KNO$_3$ in 250 g H$_2$O. *Hint:* Convert the concentrations to the proper units for solubility before referring to the graph.

7. Define the terms saturated, unsaturated, and supersaturated as they apply to solutions. Use complete sentences.

Teachers who have access to computer-based graphing programs (such as Vernier's Graphical Analysis Software, Flinn Catalog No. TC1404) may want to schedule additional lab time for students to graph their data. Students may notice (and point out to their teachers) that they are plotting the independent variable on the y-axis. This is opposite what they are normally instructed and expected to do!

Solubility and Temperature – Page 6

8. Based on your graph, classify each of the following solutions as either unsaturated or supersaturated at the indicated temperature. Assume that the solutions do not contain any undissolved solid. (a) 75 g KNO_3 in 100 g H_2O at 40 °C; (b) 60 g of KNO_3 in 50 g H_2O at 80 °C. Explain your reasoning.

9. Some of the water may have evaporated from the test tubes before their saturation temperatures were measured. What effect would this error have on the solubility of potassium nitrate for a solution? Would the corresponding saturation temperature be too high or too low as a result of this error?

10. All thermometers have a lag time—it takes a little while to register or report a temperature change. What effect would this error have on the solubility of potassium nitrate for a solution? Would the corresponding saturation temperature be too high or too low as a result of this error?

Teacher Notes

Teacher's Notes
Solubility and Temperature

Master Materials List *(for a class of 28 students working in groups of four)*

Potassium nitrate, KNO_3, about 45 g	Beakers, 50- and 250-mL, 7 each
Distilled or deionized water	Beral-type pipets, thin stem, 15
Balances, centigram precision, 3	Test tubes, 13 × 100 mm, 45
Gloves, heat-resistant, or Heat protectors, 7	Test tube clamps or holders, 15
Hot plate, 7	Thermometers, digital, 15
Spatulas, 15	Wax pencils or labeling pens, 15

Safety Precautions

Potassium nitrate in solid form is a strong oxidant and a fire and explosion risk when heated or in contact with organic materials. It is also a skin irritant. Avoid contact with skin and eyes. Wear chemical splash goggles and chemical-resistant gloves and apron. Use caution when working with a hot water bath and a hot plate. Wear heat-resistant gloves or a heat protector when handling hot glassware. Remind students to wash their hands thoroughly with soap and water before leaving the laboratory. Please consult current Material Safety Data Sheets for additional safety, handling, and disposal information.

Disposal

Consult your current *Flinn Scientific Catalog/Reference Manual* for general guidelines and specific procedures governing the disposal of laboratory waste. Potassium nitrate solutions may be rinsed down the drain with excess water according to Flinn Suggested Disposal Method #26b. Alternatively, the solutions may be collected in a central location and allowed to evaporate. The solid potassium nitrate remaining after solvent evaporation may be recrystalized for use by another class or for the following year.

Lab Hints

- The laboratory work for this experiment can reasonably be completed in one 50-minute lab period. The *Pre-Lab Questions* may be assigned as homework in preparation for lab or they may be used as the basis of a cooperative class discussion before lab.

- Adjust the working group size and the number of samples each group tests to accommodate your lab setting and schedule. The experiment as written calls for each pair of students to test three solutions and share their data with another pair of students in the same working group. Doing the experiment this way gives six data points for the solubility curve. The solubility trend is apparent with as few as four data points, but the best-fit curved line will give better agreement with the literature if more points are used. Teachers should grade more by the shape of the solubility curve than by the solubility values. Alternatively, the experiment may be done as a cooperative activity by plotting class data. This approach may give the best overall fit for the solubility curve.

- Have students use warm tap water in their water baths. This will help speed up the heating process and save time. Remind students not to boil the water in their hot water bath. Temperatures of 80–90 °C work well.

Digital thermometers are preferred in this microscale experiment. With less than 1 mL of water in each test tube, there is not enough liquid volume to immerse the bulb of a conventional bulb thermometer. Digital thermometers are also much more responsive and therefore give better data than do the regular thermometers. If digital thermometers are not available, consider scaling up the reactants (potassium nitrate and water) twofold.

Teacher's Notes

- If ice is available in the lab, students may extend the solubility curve downward below room temperature by decreasing the mass of potassium nitrate. Use mass ratios of 0.20–0.30 g KNO$_3$ per gram of water to obtain saturation temperatures between 0 and 20 °C. Adding a couple of data points in this temperature range will improve the fit between the literature and the experimental solubility curve.

- Distribute magnifying glasses, if available, to help students observe the first signs of crystal formation. Test tubes must be clean for best results. We recommend using reagent rather than laboratory grade potassium nitrate for this experiment. The potassium nitrate may be recovered from the solutions and recrystalized for use in subsequent years.

- Other solids may also be used in this experiment. The solubility curve of ammonium chloride is similar in shape (exponential) to that of potassium nitrate, but not as steep (see the *Answers to the Pre-Lab Questions* for a sample graph). Use 0.35–0.65 g of ammonium chloride per gram of water to obtain saturation temperatures between 20 and 80 °C. The solubility curve of potassium chloride in water is approximately linear. Masses of solute between 0.35 and 0.50 g per gram of water are suitable for measuring the solubility of potassium chloride in water.

- Expect quite a bit of scatter in the saturation temperature measurements obtained by different student groups. The *Supplementary Information* section has a sample graph that shows both literature data and typical classroom data for the solubility of potassium nitrate.

Teaching Tip

- The temperature dependence of solubility depends on whether the heat of solution is exothermic or endothermic. For many (although not all) ionic compounds, the heat of solution is endothermic and their solubility increases as the temperature increases. The amount of heat absorbed or released when an ionic compound dissolves in water determines the effect of temperature on the solubility of the salt. Whether heat is absorbed or released depends on both the energy required to disrupt the crystal structure of the ionic solid and the energy liberated when the cations and anions interact with the solvent. This experiment may be referred to again when equilibrium is introduced—the temperature dependence of solubility may be explained in terms of LeChâtelier's Principle and the effect of temperature on the equilibrium constant for the reaction (the solubility product constant).

Answers to Pre-Lab Questions *(Student answers will vary.)*

1. Many solutes, including potassium nitrate, have a tendency to remain in solution even after it has been cooled to below the saturation point. This phenomenon is known as supersaturation. Read the entire *Procedure* carefully. What measure is taken to prevent supersaturation during this experiment?

    Supersaturation occurs when there are no sites for crystal formation in a hot, unstirred solution. Stir the solution continuously with the thermometer to provide agitation and stimulate crystal formation. **Note to teachers:** *Using old test tubes with a scratch or two will also prevent supersaturation. Do not stir using a regular, glass-bulb thermometer.*

Teacher Notes

Strictly speaking, the effect of temperature on solubility depends on the "differential heat of solution" at saturation. This is not the same as the heat of solution obtained in a typical calorimetry experiment.

Flinn ChemTopic™ Labs — Solubility and Solutions

Teacher's Notes

Teacher Notes

2. A mixture containing 2.75 g of ammonium chloride (NH_4Cl) in 5.0 g of water was heated to dissolve the solid and then allowed to cool in air. At 61 °C, the first crystals appeared in solution. What is the solubility of ammonium chloride (in g of NH_4Cl per 100 g of water) at 61 °C?

The ratio of the mass of solute to the mass of solvent is (2.75 g/5.0 g) or 0.55 g of NH_4Cl per gram of H_2O. Multiply this ratio by 100 to obtain the solubility in the desired units of grams of solute per 100 grams of solvent. The solubility of ammonium chloride is 55 g NH_4Cl per 100 g of water at 61 °C.

$$\frac{2.75 \text{ g } NH_4Cl}{5.0 \text{ g } H_2O} = \frac{55 \text{ g } NH_4Cl}{100 \text{ g } H_2O}$$

3. The solubility of ammonium chloride in water was measured as described in this experiment and graphed as follows. Use the solubility curve to predict the solubility of ammonium chloride in water at 40 °C.

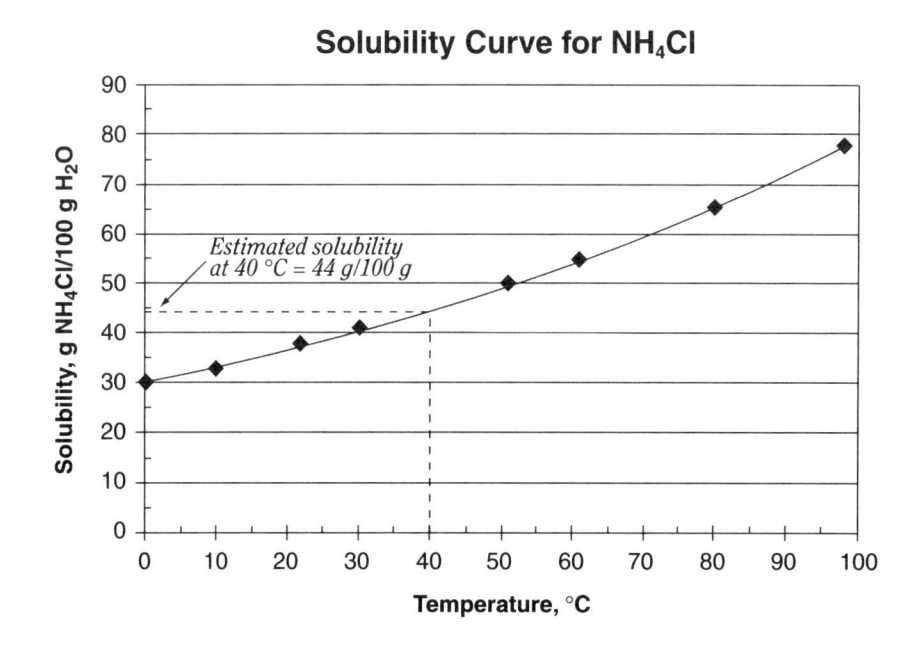

Solubility Curve for NH_4Cl

Estimated solubility at 40 °C = 44 g/100 g

To estimate the solubility of the solute at a specific temperature, draw a straight line from the temperature on the x-axis to the best-fit curved line through the data. Follow this point across horizontally to where it crosses the y-axis. The solubility of ammonium chloride at 40 °C is approximately 44 g per 100 g of water.

4. One of the students doing the experiment only had time to measure the saturation temperatures for three solutions at 51 °C, 61 °C, and 80 °C, respectively. Looking at the graph, do you think the student would have been able to accurately predict the shape of the solubility curve based on these three points? Explain.

Using only three data points, the student might have incorrectly concluded that the relationship between solubility and temperature was linear (followed a straight line). Ideally, the solubility of a substance in water should be measured over its entire liquid range.

Teacher's Notes

Sample Data

Student data will vary.

Data Table

Sample		Mass of empty test tube	Mass of test tube plus KNO_3	Mass of test tube plus KNO_3 plus water	Saturation temperature
Series I	A	5.30 g	5.80 g	6.77 g	30.9 °C
	B	5.29 g	6.04 g	6.95 g	46.2 °C
	C	5.31 g	6.54 g	7.51 g	62.6 °C
Series II	A	5.26 g	5.62 g	6.52 g	25.5 °C
	B	5.31 g	6.25 g	7.24 g	51.5 °C
	C	5.29 g	6.82 g	7.77 g	77.0 °C

Answers to Post-Lab Calculations and Analysis *(Student answers will vary.)*

1. Calculate the mass of potassium nitrate and the mass of water in each solution.

    For sample I-A: Mass of KNO_3 = 5.80 − 5.30 = 0.50 g

    Mass of H_2O = 6.77 − 5.80 = 0.97 g

    See the **Sample Results Table** on page 35 for the results of other calculations.

2. Calculate the ratio of the mass of potassium nitrate to the mass of water for each solution.

    For sample I-A: Mass ratio KNO_3/H_2O = 0.50 g/0.97 g = 0.52

    See the **Sample Results Table** on page 35 for the results of other calculations.

3. Multiply the mass ratio by 100 to determine the concentration of each saturated solution in grams of potassium nitrate per 100 grams of water.

    For sample I-A: 0.52 × 100 = 52 g KNO_3 in 100 g H_2O

    See the **Sample Results Table** on page 35 for the results of other calculations.

Teacher's Notes

Sample Results Table

Sample	Mass of KNO$_3$	Mass of H$_2$O	Mass Ratio	Solubility g KNO$_3$/100 g H$_2$O	Saturation temperature
I-A	0.50 g	0.97g	0.52	52	30.9 °C
I-B	0.75 g	0.91 g	0.82	82	46.2 °C
I-C	1.23 g	0.97 g	1.27	127	62.6 °C
II-A	0.36 g	0.90 g	0.40	40	25.5 °C
II-B	0.94 g	0.99 g	0.95	95	51.5 °C
II-C	1.53 g	0.95 g	1.61	161	77.0 °C

4. Plot a graph of solubility of potassium nitrate (in g of solute/100 g of water) on the y-axis versus temperature on the x-axis. Scale each axis as necessary. Draw a smooth, best-fit *curved line* though the data points. Don't forget to label each axis and give the graph a title!

Solubility Curve – Potassium Nitrate

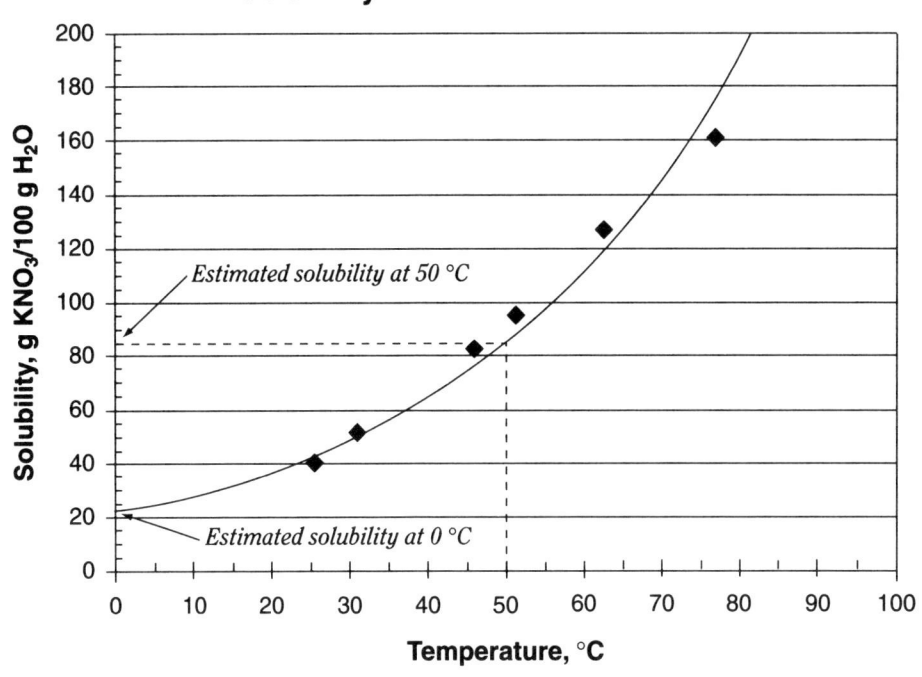

5. Using your graph, estimate the solubility of potassium nitrate in water at (a) 0 °C; (b) 50 °C; and (c) 100 °C.

Estimated solubility of potassium nitrate: *(a) 22 g KNO$_3$/100 g H$_2$O at 0 °C*
                                                                        (b) 85 g KNO$_3$/100 g H$_2$O at 50 °C
                                                                        (c) >200 g KNO$_3$/100 g H$_2$O at 100 °C
                                                                            (off-scale on above graph!)

Teacher's Notes

6. Using your graph, predict the temperature at which each of the following mixtures of potassium nitrate in water would form a saturated solution: (a) 25 g KNO₃ in 25 g H₂O; (b) 100 g KNO₃ in 250 g H₂O. *Hint:* Convert the concentrations to the proper units for solubility before referring to the graph.

Solution concentration	Solubility units	Saturation temperature
25 g KNO₃/25 g H₂O	100 g KNO₃/100 g H₂O	55 °C
100 g KNO₃/250 g H₂O	40 g KNO₃/100 g H₂O	22 °C

7. Define the terms saturated, unsaturated, and supersaturated as they apply to solutions. Use complete sentences.

   A saturated solution contains the maximum amount of solute that will dissolve in a given amount of solvent at a particular temperature. A saturated solution usually contains some undissolved solid indicating that no more solid will dissolve at that temperature. An unsaturated solution contains less than the maximum amount of solid that will dissolve in a solvent at a particular temperature. A supersaturated solution contains more than the maximum amount of solute that can dissolve in a given amount of solvent at a particular temperature. Assuming that sufficient time has been allowed to dissolve the solute, neither unsaturated nor supersaturated solutions should contain any undissolved solute.

8. Based on your graph, classify each of the following solutions as either unsaturated or supersaturated at the indicated temperature. Assume that the solutions do not contain any undissolved solid. (a) 75 g KNO₃ in 100 g H₂O at 40 °C; (b) 60 g of KNO₃ in 50 g H₂O at 80 °C. Explain your reasoning.

   (a) *A data point corresponding to a solubility of 75 g KNO₃ per 100 g H₂O and a temperature of 40 °C lies above the best-fit solubility curve drawn through the data points in the sample graph. This solution contains more than the maximum amount of solute that should dissolve at this temperature and would therefore be classified as a supersaturated solution.*

   (b) *A data point corresponding to 60 g KNO₃ per 50 g H₂O (120 g KNO₃/100 g H₂O) and a temperature of 80 °C lies below the best-fit solubility curve in the sample graph. The solution contains less than the maximum amount of solute that should dissolve at this temperature and is unsaturated.*

   See the graph on page 37.

Teacher Notes

Solubility Curve – Potassium Nitrate

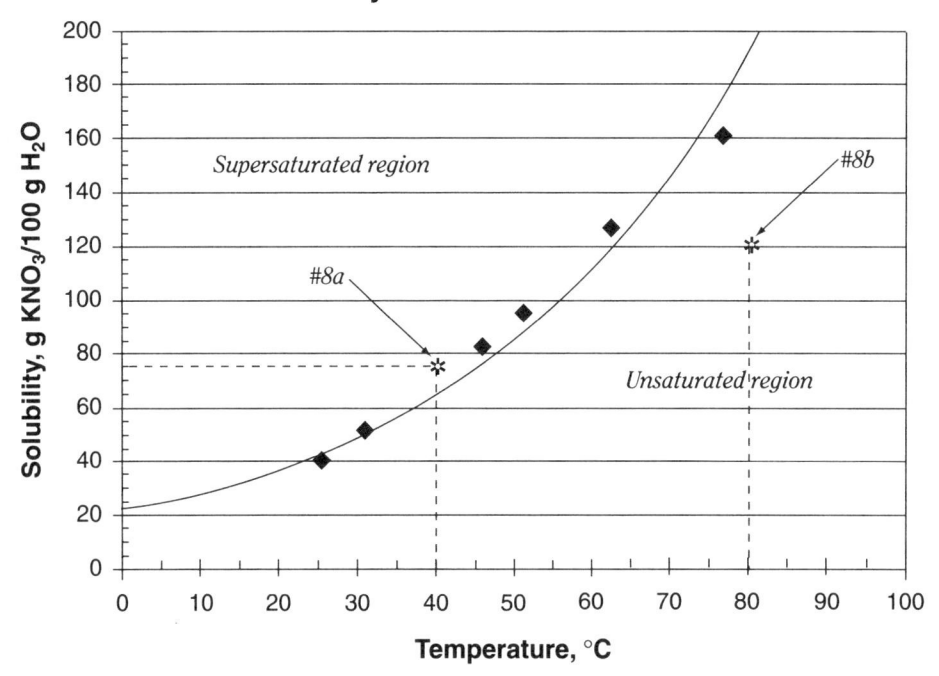

[Graph showing solubility (g KNO₃/100 g H₂O) vs Temperature (°C). Data points follow a curve rising from about 20 g at 0°C to about 160 g at 80°C. Regions labeled "Supersaturated region" (above curve) and "Unsaturated region" (below curve). Point #8a marked at approximately 40°C, 75 g. Point #8b marked at approximately 80°C, 120 g.]

9. Some of the water may have evaporated from the test tubes before their saturation temperatures were measured. What effect would this error have on the solubility of potassium nitrate for a solution? Would the corresponding saturation temperature be too high or too low as a result of this error?

   *The concentration in the test tube would be greater than the calculated value because the same amount of solute would be dissolved in a smaller amount of water. The saturation temperature that was measured would be too high for the **calculated** concentration of the solute.*

10. All thermometers have a lag time—it takes a little while to register or report a temperature change. What effect would this error have on the solubility of potassium nitrate for a solution? Would the corresponding saturation temperature be too high or too low as a result of this error?

    The thermometer response time would have no effect on the calculated concentration (solubility) of potassium nitrate. The saturation temperature that would be measured for the calculated solubility would be too high, however, as a result of this error. Remember, the temperature is measured as the solution cools.

Teacher's Notes

Supplementary Information

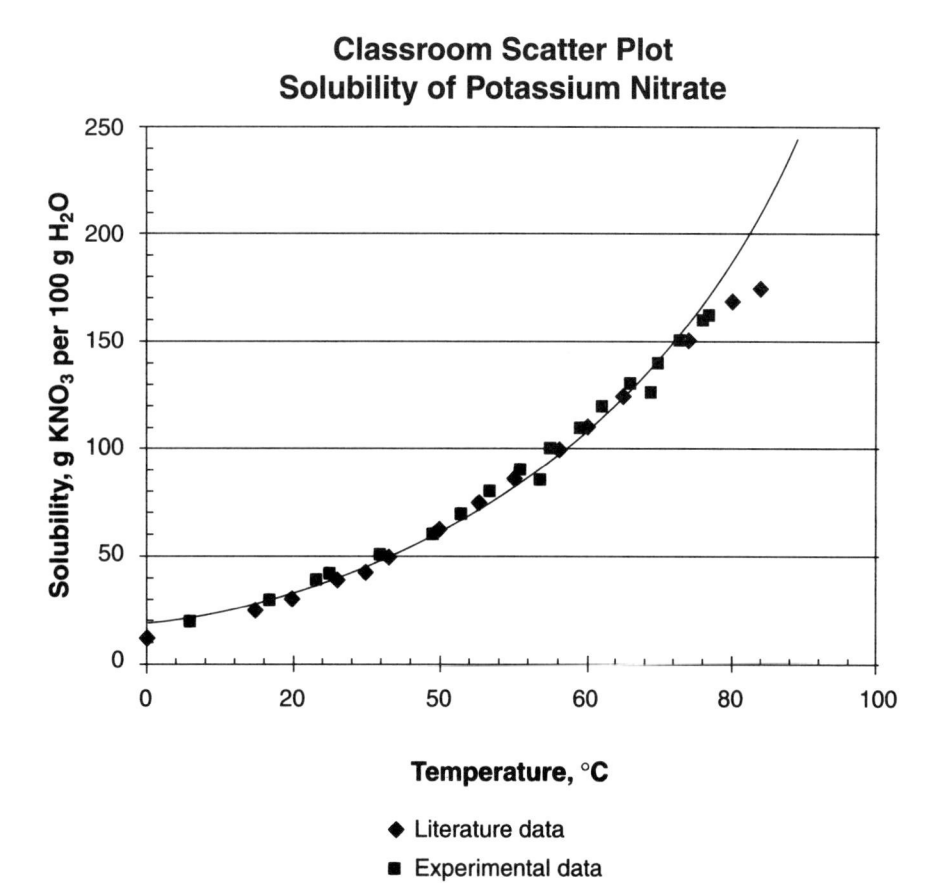

**Classroom Scatter Plot
Solubility of Potassium Nitrate**

X-axis: Temperature, °C
Y-axis: Solubility, g KNO₃ per 100 g H₂O

◆ Literature data
■ Experimental data

Teacher Notes

Preparing and Diluting Solutions
Concentration and Absorbance

Introduction

Solutions are an important part of chemistry. But how are accurate concentrations of solutions prepared? In this laboratory activity, a copper(II) sulfate solution will first be prepared, then diluted to prepare several other solutions with different concentrations.

Concepts

- Concentration
- Molarity
- Dilution equation
- Absorbance

Background

The amount of solute that is dissolved in a given quantity of solvent is called the concentration of the solution. A dilute solution contains only a small amount of solute in a given amount of solution, while a concentrated solution contains a large amount of solute in a given amount of solution. Molarity is the unit most commonly used to describe the concentration of a solution. The molarity, M, of a solution is defined as the number of moles of solute in one liter of solution (Equation 1).

$$\text{Molarity} = \frac{\text{amount of solute in moles}}{\text{volume of solution in liters}} \qquad \textit{Equation 1}$$

Combined with the molar mass of a solute, Equation 1 is used to calculate the number of grams of solute needed to prepare a given volume of a solution with a specific concentration. For example, consider the preparation of 500.0 mL of a 0.80 M solution of sodium chloride:

Step 1—Determine the number of moles necessary to prepare the solution.

$$\text{moles of solute} = \text{Molarity} \times \text{volume of solution}$$

$$\text{moles of NaCl} = \frac{0.80 \text{ moles NaCl}}{1 \text{ L}} \times 500.0 \text{ mL} \times \frac{1 \text{ L}}{1000 \text{ mL}}$$

$$\text{moles of NaCl} = 0.40 \text{ mole}$$

Step 2—Convert the number of moles to grams using the molar mass.

$$\text{grams of solute} = \text{moles of solute} \times \text{molar mass of solute}$$

$$\text{grams of NaCl} = 0.40 \text{ mole} \times \frac{58.5 \text{ g}}{1 \text{ mole}}$$

$$\text{grams of NaCl} = 23 \text{ g}$$

The calculations show that 23 g of sodium chloride are required to prepare 500.0 mL of 0.80 M NaCl solution.

Preparing and Diluting Solutions – Page 2

Once the calculations have been done to determine how much solute is needed to prepare a solution, precise analytical techniques must be followed to ensure accuracy in making the solution. Part A in the *Procedure* section describes in detail the proper analytical procedure for preparing a solution.

One very important aspect of analytical technique involves choosing the right type of glassware. Volumetric glassware is glassware that has been calibrated (and marked) to hold a specific volume. The most common form of volumetric glassware used for preparing solutions is the volumetric flask (Figure 1), which has a long, narrow neck with a single, hairline marking on it. For a 100-mL volumetric flask, the mark on the neck indicates that when filled to the mark, the flask will contain precisely 100.0 mL at room temperature.

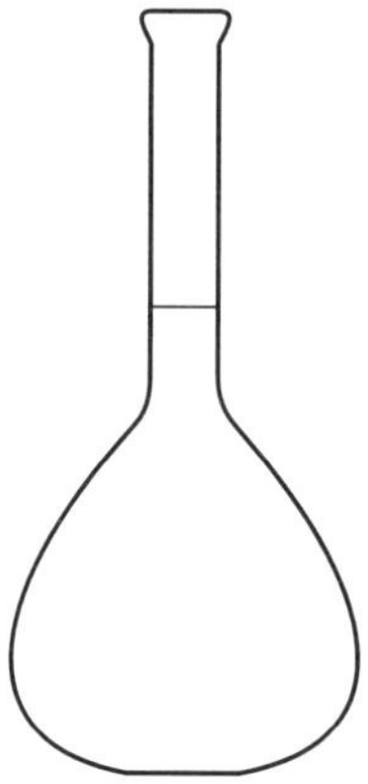

Figure 1.

Diluting Solutions

Experiments often require a solution that is more dilute than what is on hand in the stockroom. In this case, a more concentrated stock solution must be diluted to obtain the desired concentration. To carry out a dilution, the following equation is used:

$$\text{Molarity}_{\text{concentrated soln}} \times \text{volume}_{\text{concentrated soln}} = \text{Molarity}_{\text{dilute soln}} \times \text{volume}_{\text{dilute soln}}$$

In this equation, Molarity$_{\text{concentrated soln}}$ is the concentration of the stock solution, volume$_{\text{concentrated soln}}$ is the volume of the stock solution required to prepare the dilute solution, Molarity$_{\text{dilute soln}}$ is the concentration of the desired dilute solution, and volume$_{\text{dilute soln}}$ is the volume of the dilute solution needed. The dilution equation is commonly written as shown in Equation 2. The subscripts 1 and 2 refer to the concentrated solution and the dilute solution, respectively.

$$M_1 V_1 = M_2 V_2 \qquad \textit{Equation 2}$$

For example, assume that the 0.80 M sodium chloride solution prepared in the example above is in the stockroom, but for another experiment, 100 mL of a 0.20 M sodium chloride solution is needed. In performing a dilution calculation, M_1, M_2, and V_2 are generally known and Equation 2 is rearranged to solve for the unknown V_1. Substituting the known values for this example into Equation 2 allows us to solve for the volume of the concentrated solution required to prepare the dilute solution.

$$V_1 = \frac{M_2 V_2}{M_1}$$

$$V_1 = \frac{0.20 \text{ M} \times 100 \text{ mL}}{0.80 \text{ M}}$$

$$V_1 = 25 \text{ mL}$$

Proper analytical technique for preparing the diluted solution requires that the initial and final volumes (V_1 and V_2) must be accurately measured using a graduated cylinder or, preferably, a pipet and a volumetric flask.

Teacher Notes

Because volumetric flasks are expensive, they may not be available for every student lab group. However, solutions are not commonly stored in volumetric flasks, so only a few volumetric flasks are necessary for an entire class to prepare solutions.

Teacher Notes

Concentration and Absorbance

Molarity and dilution calculations show us how to prepare solutions of known concentration. Another important problem chemists encounter in the lab is how to determine the concentration of an unknown solution. If the solution is colored, the concentration of an unknown solution can be determined by measuring the intensity of the color. A special sensor or instrument called a colorimeter is used to measure the absorbance of visible light that gives the solution its color. Generally, the more intense the color of the solution, the greater the absorbance of light will be. In using colorimetry, it is important to remember that the color of light transmitted by the solution (the color we see) is complementary to the color of light absorbed by the solution (the color we measure). Since the color of light depends on its wavelength, the wavelength of light absorbed by a colored substance in solution is complementary to the wavelength of light transmitted by the substance. Copper(II) sulfate solutions, for example, are blue. The absorbance of copper(II) sulfate solutions is measured at 635 nm, corresponding to red light.

Experiment Overview

The purpose of this experiment is to prepare a series of blue copper(II) sulfate solutions of known concentration using the molarity and dilution equations. The relationship between the concentration of a solution and its absorbance will be investigated. The accuracy of the solution preparation and dilution procedures will then be determined.

Pre-Lab Questions

1. Calculate the number of grams of copper(II) sulfate pentahydrate, $CuSO_4 \cdot 5H_2O$, required to prepare 100.0 mL of a 0.150 M copper(II) sulfate solution.

2. Calculate the number of milliliters of 0.150 M copper(II) sulfate solution that must be diluted to prepare 10.0 mL of a 0.0750 M copper(II) sulfate solution.

3. Calculate the number of milliliters of 0.150 M copper(II) sulfate solution that must be diluted to prepare 10.0 mL of a 0.0230 M copper(II) sulfate solution.

Materials

Copper(II) sulfate pentahydrate, $CuSO_4 \cdot 5H_2O$, 3 g
Balance, centigram precision
Beaker, 250-mL
Beral-type pipets, 6
Bottle, plastic, with cap, 150-mL or larger
Colorimeter or spectrophotometer
Computer interface system (LabPro™)
Computer or calculator for data collection
Cuvets, 5
Data collection software (LoggerPro™)
Funnel

Graduated cylinder, 10-mL
Paper towels
Spatula
Stirring rod
Test tube rack
Test tubes, 16 × 125 mm, 5
Tissues or lens paper
Volumetric flask, 100-mL
Wash bottle filled with distilled or deionized water
Water, distilled or deionized
Wax pencil or labeling tape
Weighing dish

Preparing and Diluting Solutions – Page 4

Safety Precautions

Copper(II) sulfate is moderately toxic by ingestion and inhalation and is a skin and respiratory irritant. Avoid contact with eyes and skin. Wear chemical splash goggles, chemical-resistant gloves, and a chemical-resistant apron. Wash hands thoroughly with soap and water before leaving the laboratory.

Procedure

Part A. Preparing the Stock Solution

1. Review the calculations from *Pre-Lab Question* #1 for the number of grams of copper(II) sulfate pentahydrate, $CuSO_4 \cdot 5H_2O$, required to prepare 100.0 mL of a 0.150 M solution. Check them with your instructor. Once your calculations have been approved, weigh out the required amount of copper sulfate on a balance in a clean, dry weighing dish.

2. Transfer the solid to a clean, dry beaker. Use a wash bottle filled with distilled or deionized water to rinse any remaining solid from the weighing dish into the beaker.

3. Dissolve the solid in the beaker in a minimum amount of distilled or deionized water, then transfer the solution to a 100-mL volumetric flask using a funnel. Rinse the beaker with distilled or deionized water using a wash bottle. Pour the rinse water through the funnel and into the volumetric flask so that every bit of solution is transferred to the volumetric flask.

4. Slowly add more distilled or deionized water to the volumetric flask until the flask is two-thirds full. Place the cap on the volumetric flask and invert it several times to mix the solution. Continue filling the flask until the liquid level is almost to the 100-mL mark. Fill to the mark with a pipet or wash bottle drop-by-drop so that no water splashes up on the sides of the flask. Fill until the bottom of the meniscus is exactly at the 100.0-mL mark.

5. Cap the volumetric flask and invert it 10–15 times to give a homogeneous solution.

6. Once the solution is thoroughly mixed, transfer it to a clean, labeled bottle. Cap the bottle to prevent evaporation or contamination of the solution. Clean and put away the volumetric flask.

Part B. Preparing Diluted Solutions

7. Place five clean and dry test tubes in a test tube rack and label them #1–5. Label one pipet "$CuSO_4$" and use it to transfer the stock solution only.

8. Using a 10-mL graduated cylinder, measure and pour 10 mL of the 0.150 M stock solution into test tube #1. Record the necessary data for this solution in the data table.

9. Using a clean Beral-type pipet, fill the 10-mL graduated cylinder exactly to the 3.80-mL mark with the stock solution. Try not to get any drops of solution on the sides of the cylinder. Make sure that the bottom of the meniscus sits exactly at the 3.80-mL mark.

10. Carefully fill the graduated cylinder to the 10.0-mL mark with distilled or deionized water. Do not overfill!

Teacher Notes

In Part B, proper analytical technique would require the use of calibrated pipets and volumetric flasks. The availability of a classroom set of these might be prohibitive. Graduated cylinders are sufficient for the precision reported in this experiment.

*Page 5 – **Preparing and Diluting Solutions***

Teacher Notes

11. Mix the solution in the graduated cylinder by repeatedly filling and emptying a clean pipet with the solution three times. The agitation caused by filling and emptying the pipet will mix the solution.

12. Transfer the mixed solution to test tube #2 and record the necessary data for this solution in the data table.

13. Rinse the graduated cylinder with water and dry it with a paper towel.

14. Repeat steps 9–11 using 2.40 mL of stock solution.

15. Transfer the mixed solution to test tube #3 and record the necessary data for this solution in the data table.

16. Rinse the graduated cylinder with water and dry it with a paper towel.

17. Before proceeding, review your calculations for preparation of 10.0 mL of a 0.075 M and a 0.023 M cupric sulfate solution (*Pre-Lab Questions* #2 and #3). Check with your instructor before proceeding.

18. Using your calculations and the analytical technique described in steps 9–13, prepare 10.0 mL of a 0.075 M cupric sulfate solution by diluting the stock solution. Transfer this solution to test tube #4 and record the necessary data in the data table.

19. Using your calculations and the analytical technique described in steps 9–13, prepare 10.0 mL of a 0.023 M cupric sulfate solution by diluting the stock solution. Transfer this solution to test tube #5 and record the necessary data in the data table.

20. Compare the color of the stock solution and each of the dilutions in test tubes #1–5. Rank them in terms of color from deepest blue to lightest blue. Record these observations in the data table.

Part C. Colorimetry Measurements

21. Rinse five cuvets with about 1 mL of the solutions from Part B, then fill the cuvets with each solution. Arrange the cuvets in order (#1–5) on a *labeled* sheet of paper to keep track of the solutions. Do not write on the cuvets.

22. Handle the cuvets by their ribbed sides or their tops to avoid getting fingerprints on the surface. Wipe the cuvets with lint-free tissue paper or lens paper.

23. Connect the interface system to the computer or calculator and plug the colorimeter sensor into the interface.

24. Select *Setup* and *Sensors* from the main screen and choose "Colorimeter."

Note: Many newer sensors have an automatic calibration feature that automatically calibrates the colorimeter before use. If the sensor has the autocalibration feature, proceed directly to step 29. If not, follow steps 25–28 to calibrate the colorimeter for 100% transmission (0 absorbance) with a "blank" cuvet containing only distilled water.

Part C may also be carried out using a spectrophotometer. If fewer than five cuvets are available per lab group, instruct students to fill a cuvet and test the solutions in order from least concentrated to most concentrated.

Preparing and Diluting Solutions – Page 6

Teacher Notes

25. Select *Calibrate* and *Perform Now* from the Experiment menu on the main screen.

26. Fill a cuvet about ¾ full with distilled water. Wipe the cuvet with a lint-free tissue, then place the cuvet in the colorimeter compartment.

27. Set the wavelength knob on the colorimeter to 0%T—the onscreen box should read zero. Press *Keep* when the voltage is steady.

28. Turn the wavelength knob on the colorimeter to 635 nm (red)—the onscreen box should read 100. Press *Keep* when the voltage is steady.

29. Return to the main screen and set up a live readout and data table that will record absorbance (as a function of time).

30. Select *Setup* followed by *Data Collection*. Click on *Selected Events* to set the computer for manual sampling.

31. Remove the "blank" cuvet from the colorimeter compartment and replace it with the cuvet containing solution #1.

32. Press *Collect* on the main screen to begin absorbance measurements.

33. When the absorbance reading stabilizes, press *Keep* on the main screen to automatically record the absorbance measurement. *Note:* The absorbance measurement should appear in a data table onscreen. The onscreen data table will also contain a time reading, which may be ignored.

34. Remove the cuvet from the colorimeter compartment and replace it with the cuvet containing solution #2.

35. When the absorbance reading stabilizes, press *Keep* on the main screen to automatically record the absorbance measurement.

36. Repeat steps 34 and 35 with the other solutions #3–5.

37. Press *Stop* on the main screen to end the data collection process. If possible, obtain a printout of the data table.

38. Record the absorbance data for solutions #1–5 in the Data Table.

39. Dispose of the contents of the cuvets and of the remaining test solutions as directed by your instructor.

40. Follow your instructor's directions for rinsing and drying the cuvets.

Page 7 – **Preparing and Diluting Solutions**

Teacher Notes

Name: _____

Class/Lab Period: _____

Preparing and Diluting Solutions

Data Table

Test Tube	1*	2	3	4	5
Volume of Stock Solution (V_1)					
Concentration of Stock Solution (M_1)					
Final Volume of Diluted Solution (V_2)					
Concentration of Diluted Solution (M_2)					
Color Comparison (Rank solutions from lightest blue = 1, deepest blue = 5)					
Absorbance at 635 nm					

*Test tube #1 contains the initial stock solution.

Post-Lab Questions *(Use a separate sheet of paper to answer the following questions.)*

1. Calculate the concentrations of the diluted solutions in test tubes #2 and 3 using Equation 2 from the *Background* section.

2. Complete the data table for test tubes #1, 4, and 5. *Note:* See the *Pre-Lab Questions* for the calculated values for solutions #4 and 5.

3. Compare the concentration of each solution to the color ranking. What is the relationship between the concentration of a solution and its color intensity?

4. Compare the concentration of each solution with its absorbance. What is the relationship between concentration and absorbance?

5. Obtain or prepare a graph of absorbance on the y-axis versus the concentration of each solution on the x-axis.

6. Does it make sense that the relationship between concentration and absorbance should include the origin (0,0) as a point? Explain your reasoning.

7. Based on your answer to Question #6, draw the "best-fit" straight line through the data points. How well does this straight line fit the data? Describe the accuracy of the relationship between concentration and absorbance.

8. The absorbance of a copper(II) sulfate solution of unknown concentration was measured by colorimetry and found to be 0.250. Use your graph of absorbance versus concentration to estimate the concentration of this unknown solution.

For best results, have students prepare graphs using the data collection software (LoggerPro™) or a graphical analysis program.

Preparing and Diluting Solutions

Teacher's Notes
Preparing and Diluting Solutions

Master Materials List *(for a class of 30 students working in pairs)*

Copper(II) sulfate, $CuSO_4 \cdot 5H_2O$, 50 g	Paper towels
Balances, centigram precision, 3	Spatulas, 15
Beakers, 250-mL, 15	Stirring rods, 15
Beral-type pipets, 75	Test tube racks, 15
Bottles, plastic, with cap, 150-mL, 15	Test tubes, 16 × 125 mm, 60
Colorimeters or spectrophotometer, 15	Tissues or lens paper
Computer interface systems (LabPro), 15	Volumetric flasks, 100-mL, 5–7
Computer or calculator for data collection	Wash bottles, 15
Cuvets, 75	Water, distilled or deionized
Data collection software (LoggerPro)	Wax pencils or labeling tape, 15
Funnels, 15	Weighing dishes, 15
Graduated cylinders, 10-mL, 15	

Safety Precautions

Cupric sulfate is moderately toxic by ingestion and inhalation and is a skin and respiratory irritant. Avoid contact with eyes and skin. Wear chemical splash goggles, chemical-resistant gloves, and a chemical-resistant apron. Remind students to wash their hands thoroughly with soap and water before leaving the laboratory. Please consult current Material Safety Data Sheets for additional safety, handling, and disposal information.

Disposal

Consult your current *Flinn Scientific Catalog/Reference Manual* for general guidelines and specific procedures governing the disposal of laboratory waste. Waste copper(II) sulfate solutions may be disposed of down the drain with plenty of excess water according to Flinn Suggested Disposal Method #26b.

Lab Hints

- The laboratory work for this experiment will probably require two 50-minute lab periods for completion. This is a large time investment, but the experiment introduces many valuable skills—concentration calculations, analytical technique, and colorimetry.

- Volumetric flasks are the best type of glassware in which to prepare a solution. However, because they are so expensive, they may not be available for each student group. If you have just a few volumetric flasks, have students take turns using them. Once their solution is prepared, students should transfer it to a labeled bottle and pass the volumetric flask on to the next group.

- If there are not enough volumetric flasks available to share among the class, have students calibrate an Erlenmeyer flask or a square dropping bottle using a graduated cylinder.

Teacher's Notes

Teacher Notes

- Copper(II) sulfate pentahydrate is available in both laboratory and reagent grade and in several crystal sizes. For best results, we recommend using the reagent chemical only, fine crystal grade. Using the fine crystal grade will ensure that the copper sulfate dissolves easily and readily. The reagent material should give a better straight line relationship between concentration and absorbance.

Teaching Tip

- This lab may be upgraded for honors or advanced chemistry classes. Give students unknowns to analyze by colorimetry or ask them to determine the percent $CuSO_4$ in laboratory-grade copper sulfate pentahydrate using this technique.

Answers to Pre-Lab Questions *(Student answers will vary.)*

1. Calculate the number of grams of copper(II) sulfate pentahydrate, $CuSO_4 \cdot 5H_2O$, required to prepare 100.0 mL of a 0.150 M copper(II) sulfate solution.

   moles of solute = Molarity × volume of solution

   $$moles\ of\ CuSO_4 \cdot 5H_2O = \frac{0.150\ moles\ CuSO_4 \cdot 5H_2O}{L} \times 100\ mL \times \frac{1\ L}{1000\ mL}$$

   moles of $CuSO_4 \cdot 5H_2O$ = 0.0150 moles

   grams of solute = moles of solute × molar mass of solute

   $$grams\ of\ CuSO_4 \cdot 5H_2O = 0.0150\ moles \times \frac{249.7g}{mole}$$

   grams of $CuSO_4 \cdot 5H_2O$ = 3.75 g

2. Calculate the number of milliliters of 0.150 M copper(II) sulfate solution that must be diluted to prepare 10.0 mL of a 0.0750 M copper(II) sulfate solution.

   $$V_1 = \frac{M_2 V_2}{M_1}$$

   $$V_1 = \frac{0.075\ M \times 10.0\ mL}{0.150\ M}$$

   $$V_1 = 5.0\ mL$$

3. Calculate the number of milliliters of 0.150 M copper(II) sulfate solution that must be diluted to prepare 10.0 mL of a 0.0230 M copper(II) sulfate solution.

   $$V_1 = \frac{M_2 V_2}{M_1}$$

   $$V_1 = \frac{0.023\ M \times 10.0\ mL}{0.150\ M}$$

   $$V_1 = 1.5\ mL$$

Preparing and Diluting Solutions

Teacher's Notes

Sample Data

Student data will vary.

Data Table

Test Tube	1*	2	3	4	5
Volume of Stock Solution (V_1)	10.0 mL	3.80 mL	2.40 mL	5.00 mL	1.50 mL
Concentration of Stock Solution (M_1)	0.150 M	0.150 M	0.150 M	0.150 M	0.150 M
Final Volume of Diluted Solution (V_2)		10.0 mL	10.0 mL	10.0 mL	10.0 mL
Concentration of Diluted Solution (M_2)		0.0570 M	0.0360 M	0.0750 M	0.0230 M
Color Comparison (Rank solutions from lightest blue = 1, deepest blue = 5)	5	3	2	4	1
Absorbance at 635 nm	0.335	0.117	0.079	0.157	0.043

*Test tube #1 contains the initial stock solution.

Answers to Post-Lab Questions *(Student answers will vary.)*

1. Calculate the concentrations of the diluted solutions in test tubes #2 and 3 using Equation 2 from the *Background* section.

    For test tube 2: $M_2 = \dfrac{M_1 \times V_1}{V_2} = \dfrac{0.150 \text{ M} \times 3.80 \text{ mL}}{10.0 \text{ mL}} = 0.0570 \text{ M}$

    For test tube 3: $M_2 = \dfrac{M_1 \times V_1}{V_2} = \dfrac{0.150 \text{ M} \times 2.40 \text{ mL}}{10.0 \text{ mL}} = 0.0360 \text{ M}$

2. Complete the data table for test tubes #1, 4, and 5. *Note:* See the *Pre-Lab Questions* for the calculated values for solutions #4 and 5.

    See the Answers to the PreLab Questions #2 and 3.

3. Compare the concentration of each solution to the color ranking. What is the relationship between the concentration of a solution and its color intensity?

    The solution with the highest concentration has the most intense color and the highest color comparison ranking (5). The solution with the lowest concentration has the least intense color and the lowest color ranking (1). For all of the solutions, the color intensity increases as the concentration of the solution increases.

4. Compare the concentration of each solution with its absorbance. What is the relationship between concentration and absorbance?

    The solution with the highest concentration has the highest absorbance. The solution with the lowest concentration has the lowest absorbance. For all of the solutions, the absorbance increases as the concentration of the solution increases.

Teacher's Notes

Teacher Notes

5. Obtain or prepare a graph of absorbance on the y-axis versus the concentration of each solution on the x-axis.

Absorbance of Copper(II) Sulfate Solutions

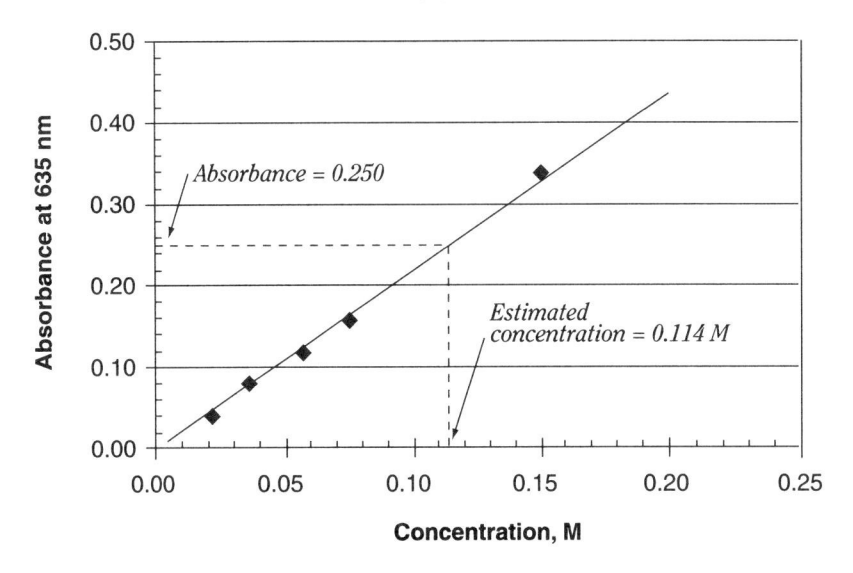

[Graph: Absorbance at 635 nm vs. Concentration, M. Data points form a straight line through the origin. Dashed lines indicate Absorbance = 0.250 corresponding to an Estimated concentration = 0.114 M.]

6. Does it make sense that the relationship between concentration and absorbance should include the origin (0,0) as a point? Explain your reasoning.

   The origin (0,0) should be included in the data points because a solution with zero concentration should be colorless and should thus have zero absorbance.

7. Based on your answer to Question #6, draw the "best-fit" straight line through the data points. How well does this straight line fit the data? Describe the accuracy of the relationship between concentration and absorbance.

   See the Sample Graph. The data show an excellent straight-line fit going through the origin. Absorbance therefore provides an accurate way to determine the concentration of a solution.

8. The absorbance of a copper(II) sulfate solution of unknown concentration was measured by colorimetry and found to be 0.250. Use your graph of absorbance versus concentration to estimate the concentration of this unknown solution.

   Read across from the absorbance (0.250) to the best-fit straight line through the data, and then downward from this point on the line to the x-axis. The place where this vertical line intersects the x-axis is the estimated concentration of the unknown solution. An absorbance of 0.250 corresponds to a concentration of 0.114 M.

Preparing and Diluting Solutions

Teacher's Notes

Page 1 – Freezing Point Depression

Teacher Notes

Freezing Point Depression
How Low Can You Go?

Introduction

People who live in northern states are familiar with winter and the snowy, icy roads that go with the season. Road crews spread salt (sodium chloride, calcium chloride or a salt mixture) on the roads in order to lower the temperature at which freezing occurs. If the road already has ice on it, the salt helps to melt the ice, forming a solution with a lower freezing point than that of pure water. Let's investigate the effect of dissolved solutes on the freezing point of a solution and determine which solute has the greatest effect on the freezing point.

Concepts

- Freezing point
- Freezing point depression
- Colligative property
- Molality

Background

The *freezing point* of a liquid is the temperature at which the forces of attraction among molecules are just great enough to cause a phase change from the liquid state to the solid state. Strictly speaking, the freezing (or melting) point of a substance is the temperature at which the liquid and solid phases are in equilibrium.

During the freezing process of water, for example, water molecules come together to form the more orderly, crystalline pattern of ice molecules. When any solute (such as salt) is added to a solvent (such as water), the crystalline pattern is interrupted by the presence of the salt "impurity." Salt and other dissolved solutes interfere with the ability of the solvent to crystallize (solidify) and the solution remains liquid even at a temperature below the freezing point of the pure solvent. Thus a solution always has a lower freezing point than its pure solvent. This phenomenon is termed freezing point depression.

Freezing point depression (ΔT_f) is defined as the difference in temperature between the freezing point of a solution and that of its pure solvent. The freezing point depression of the solution after the addition of a solute can be calculated using Equation 1.

$$\Delta T_f = K_f \times m \times i \qquad \text{Equation 1}$$

ΔT_f is the change in freezing point (the freezing point depression) in °C, K_f is the freezing point depression constant (1.86 °C/m for water solutions), m is the molality of the solution (the solution concentration in moles of solute per kilogram of solvent), and i is the number of particles formed when the solute dissolves in the solvent.

Freezing point depression is a *colligative property* of a solution. Ideally, a colligative property depends only on the number of solute particles that are formed when the solute dissolves in a given mass of solvent. It does not depend on the size or the identity of the particles. Boiling point elevation and osmotic pressure are other examples of colligative properties of a solution.

The number of solute particles obtained when a solute dissolves in water is called the van't Hoff factor (i). Experimental values of the van't Hoff factor for a solute are calculated by comparing the freezing point depression produced by a given concentration of solute to the freezing point predicted if the solute behaved as a nonelectrolyte. Using theoretical values of i in Equation 1 is valid only for ideal solutions, that is, dilute solutions where the solute particles are completely dissociated.

Freezing Point Depression – Page 2

Certain solutes lower the freezing point more than other substances. When a molecular compound such as sucrose ($C_{12}H_{22}O_{11}$) is dissolved in water, the molecules do not dissociate and remain as single particles. Ionic solutes, on the other hand, dissociate into ions when dissolved in water. Thus, one formula unit of sodium chloride (NaCl) dissociates in water to produce two particles—one sodium ion (Na^+) and one chloride ion (Cl^-). One unit of calcium chloride ($CaCl_2$) when placed in water dissociates into three particles—one calcium ion (Ca^{2+}) and two chloride ions (Cl^-). Looking at Equation 1, it can be seen that the freezing point depression depends on the number of particles in solution. The more particles in solution, the greater the change in freezing point should be.

Experiment Overview

The purpose of this experiment is to measure the freezing point of pure water and the freezing point depression for various solutions. The effect of the concentration and number of dissolved solute particles on the freezing point of water will be determined.

Pre-Lab Questions

Read the entire procedure carefully, then answer the following questions.

1. What factors will be held constant when determining the freezing point depression for each solute in this experiment?

2. Why is it important to keep the thermometer off the bottom of the beaker?

3. Why is it necessary to measure the temperature of the pure ice-water mixture, instead of assuming it to be 0.0 °C?

Materials

Aluminum chloride hexahydrate, $AlCl_3·6H_2O$, 30 g
Calcium chloride dihydrate, $CaCl_2·2H_2O$, 30 g
Sodium chloride, NaCl, 30 g
Sucrose, $C_{12}H_{22}O_{11}$, 30 g
Crushed ice, 320 g
Water, tap or distilled
Balance, 0.1 g
Beakers, 250-mL, 4
Graduated cylinder (optional)
Thermometer
Tongue depressors or plastic stirrers, 4
Weighing dishes, 4

Safety Precautions

Aluminum chloride and calcium chloride are slightly toxic by ingestion. Sodium chloride and sucrose are not considered hazardous; however, the chemicals provided are for laboratory use only and are not intended for human consumption. Avoid contact of all chemicals with eyes and skin. Wear chemical splash goggles, chemical-resistant gloves, and a chemical-resistant apron. Wash hands thoroughly with soap and water before leaving the laboratory.

Teacher Notes

*Page 3 – **Freezing Point Depression***

Teacher Notes

Procedure

Form a working group with three other students and divide into two pairs. Each pair of students will measure the freezing point of water with their thermometer (steps 2–6) and then determine the freezing point depression for two of the solutes. At the conclusion of the experiment, both pairs of students in each group will share their data and complete the data table.

1. Label four 250-mL beakers #1–4.

2. Place Beaker #1 on the balance and tare the balance, if the balance is electronic.

3. Add 100 grams of ice-water to the beaker by (a) first adding approximately 70–80 grams of crushed ice and (b) then adding enough water so the total mass of ice plus water is about 100 g. Record the precise mass of the ice-water mixture to the nearest tenth of a gram in the data table. *Note:* If the balance does not have a capacity large enough, weigh the ice in a small weighing dish and then place it in the beaker. Measure the remaining water using a balance or graduated cylinder.

4. Stir the ice-water mixture with a tongue depressor.

5. Carefully insert a thermometer into the ice-water mixture. Hold the thermometer slightly off the bottom of the beaker so that the thermometer bulb is surrounded on all sides by the ice-water mixture.

6. Wait for the temperature reading to stabilize. Record the temperature of the pure ice-water mixture in °C to the nearest tenth of a degree on the data sheet.

Beaker #1—Sodium Chloride

7. In a weighing dish, weigh out 30.0 g of sodium chloride. Record the precise mass of the sodium chloride in the data table.

8. Add the sodium chloride to the ice-water mixture in Beaker #1.

9. Stir the contents of the beaker with a tongue depressor until the mixture has a slushy appearance.

10. Carefully insert a thermometer into the mixture and measure the temperature. Stir only with the tongue depressor and not with the thermometers. Hold the thermometer in the beaker with one hand to read the temperature and stir with the wooden stirrer with the other hand.

11. Continue to stir the mixture with the tongue depressor. Record in the data table the lowest temperature (to the nearest tenth of a degree) that the mixture reaches before rising again. This may take some time, as the salt does not immediately dissolve in the ice water.

Beaker #2—Sucrose

12. Repeat steps 2–11 for Beaker #2, using 100.0 grams of ice water and 30.0 grams of sucrose. Remember to record precise masses and temperature readings to the nearest tenth of a degree.

Tongue depressors (Flinn Catalog No. AP4412) are ideal stirrers for these thick solutions, but plastic stirring rods or craft sticks may also be used. Glass stirring rods are not recommended.

Freezing Point Depression

Freezing Point Depression – *Page 4*

Beaker #3—Calcium Chloride

13. Repeat steps 2–11 for Beaker #3, using 100.0 grams of ice water and 30.0 grams of calcium chloride. Remember to record precise masses and temperature readings to the nearest tenth of a degree.

Beaker #4—Aluminum Chloride

14. Repeat steps 2–11 for Beaker #4, using 100.0 grams of ice water and 30.0 grams of aluminum chloride. Remember to record precise masses and temperature readings to the nearest tenth of a degree.

15. Dispose of the solutions by pouring the mixtures down the drain with plenty of water. Rinse the beakers with tap water.

Teacher Notes

Teacher Notes

Name: _____

Class/Lab Period: _____

Freezing Point Depression

Data Table

Freezing Point of Water _____

Beaker Number	Solute	Mass of Ice + Water	Mass of Solute	Lowest Temperature of Mixture
1	Sodium chloride, NaCl			
2	Sucrose, $C_{12}H_{22}O_{11}$			
3	Calcium chloride, $CaCl_2 \cdot 2H_2O$			
4	Aluminum chloride $AlCl_3 \cdot 6H_2O$			

Post-Lab Calculations and Analysis *(Show all work on a separate sheet of paper.)*

Fill in the results of all calculations for Questions #1–7 in the Results Table.

1. Determine the molar mass of each solute. Remember to include waters of hydration.

2. Calculate the number of moles of each solute using the exact mass of the solute from the Data Table and its molar mass.

3. Calculate the experimental value of the freezing point depression, ΔT_f for each solute, using the equation below.

$$T_f \text{ (pure solvent)} - T_f \text{ (solution)} = \Delta T_f \text{ (in °C)}$$

4. Calculate the ΔT_f per mole of solute.

5. For each solute that dissociates in water, write a balanced equation for its dissociation reaction. Determine the ideal value of i for each solute. This is the number of particles formed when one formula unit of the solute dissolves in water. *Note:* Waters of hydration are NOT included in the value of i.

6. Calculate the concentration of each solution in molality, m, defined as the number of moles of solute per kilogram of solvent.

$$\text{Molality} = m = \frac{\text{moles of solute}}{\text{kilogram of solvent}}$$

Freezing Point Depression

Freezing Point Depression – Page 6

7. Calculate the theoretical value of the freezing point depression for each solute based on the molality of the solution (*m*) and the ideal number of solute particles (*i*). Use Equation 1 from the *Background* section, K_f = 1.86 °C/*m*, and the calculated values for *m* and *i*.

8. Compare the experimental and theoretical values of ΔT_f for each solute. Discuss possible sources of error in this experiment and their likely effect on the experimental ΔT_f values.

9. Which solute had the greatest freezing point depression per mole? Which had the least? Is this what would be expected? Explain.

10. Prepare a graph of ΔT_f/mole on the y-axis versus *i* on the x-axis. Describe the relationship shown by the graph.

Results Table

Beaker Number	1	2	3	4
Solute	NaCl	$C_{12}H_{22}O_{11}$	$CaCl_2 \cdot 2H_2O$	$AlCl_3 \cdot 6H_2O$
Molar Mass (g/mole)				
Moles of Solute				
ΔT_f (exp)				
$\dfrac{\Delta T_f \text{ (exp)}}{\text{mole}}$				
i (ideal value)				
m				
ΔT_f (theor)				

Teacher Notes

Teacher Notes

Teacher's Notes
Freezing Point Depression

Master Materials List *(for a class of 28 students working in groups of four)*

Aluminum chloride hexahydrate, $AlCl_3 \cdot 6H_2O$, 210 g
Calcium chloride dihydrate, $CaCl_2 \cdot 2H_2O$, 210 g
Sodium chloride, NaCl, 210 g
Sucrose, $C_{12}H_{22}O_{11}$, 210 g
Tongue depressors or wooden stirrers, 30
Crushed ice
Balances, 3
Beakers, 250-mL, 4
Graduated cylinders (optional)
Thermometers, 15
Water, tap or distilled

Lab Hints

- The lab works significantly better with crushed ice rather than with ice cubes. If crushed ice is not available, place some ice cubes in two layers of zipper-lock bags. Using caution, pound the ice with a hammer or other hard object to crush it into small pieces.

- Have each student group use the same thermometer throughout the lab to reduce errors resulting from inaccurate thermometers.

- Distilled or deionized water will produce the best results; however, tap water may also be used as the source of water and ice in this lab. Any ions in the water will be present in every mixture, including the control, and thus should not affect comparative results. The concentration of ions in the local tap water, however, may cause the results to vary slightly from the sample data provided.

- Remind the students to use the tongue depressor to stir the solution and the thermometer strictly to measure the temperature. Also caution students not to leave thermometers standing in beakers unattended as this is a common cause of broken thermometers and spilled solutions.

- Consider providing students with an unknown salt and having them repeat the freezing point depression experiment. Have them determine i, the number of particles or ions produced from each formula unit of the unknown. Provide a list of possible unknowns.

Teaching Tips

- Given the following cost data, discuss with students which deicing chemical would be most effective or most cost-effective for preventing road icing.

Solute	Cost/kg
Sodium chloride	$ 0.64
Sucrose	$ 0.79
Calcium chloride	$ 0.77
Aluminum chloride	$ 2.76

Digital thermometers are preferred because they give faster response times, are easier to read, and will not break during vigorous stirring. Regular bulb thermometers may also be used, however.

Teacher's Notes

- This lab is designed as an introduction to colligative properties and their applications. The high concentrations of solutes used in this experiment would be expected to show fairly large deviations from ideality. The high concentrations demonstrate to students, however, just how much the freezing point of water can be lowered using simple salts. Most students are surprised to discover that they can lower the freezing point of water to almost –20 °C using just table salt. In a more rigorous advanced lab, the freezing point of a dilute solution would typically be determined by graphical analysis of a cooling curve and then used to calculate the molar mass of an unknown solute.

Answers to Pre-Lab Questions *(Student answers will vary.)*

1. What factors will be held constant when determining the freezing point depression for each solute in this experiment?

   Same thermometer throughout; same amount of ice-water mixture; same mass of solute; solutions are stirred equally throughout.

2. Why is it important to keep the thermometer off the bottom of the beaker?

   To obtain an accurate reading, the thermometer bulb should be surrounded on all sides by the solid–liquid mixture.

3. Why is it necessary to measure the temperature of the pure ice-water mixture, instead of assuming it to be 0.0 °C?

   The most important reason for measuring the freezing point of water is to calibrate the thermometer. A second reason, however, has to do with the presence of dissolved impurities in the water or ice. Local tap water supplies (which have almost certainly been used to prepare the ice) may have different water hardness values due to dissolved Mg^{2+} and Ca^{2+} ions and different alkalinity values due to dissolved carbonate (HCO_3^- and CO_3^{2-}) ions.

Teacher's Notes

Teacher Notes

Sample Data

Student data will vary.

Data Table

Freezing Point of Water ___0.0 °C___

Beaker Number	Solute	Mass of Ice + Water	Mass of Solute	Lowest Temperature of Mixture
1	Sodium chloride, NaCl	100.2 g	30.3 g	−16.7 °C
2	Sucrose, $C_{12}H_{22}O_{11}$	100.8 g	30.1 g	−1.5 °C
3	Calcium chloride, $CaCl_2 \cdot 2H_2O$	100.7 g	30.3 g	−11.5 °C
4	Aluminum chloride $AlCl_3 \cdot 6H_2O$	100.1 g	30.0 g	−11.1 °C

Answers to Post-Lab Calculations and Analysis *(Student answers will vary.)*

1. Determine the molar mass of each solute. Remember to include waters of hydration.

   Example: Molar mass of NaCl = 23.00 g/mole + 35.45 g/mole = 58.45 g/mole.

2. Calculate the number of moles of each solute using the exact mass of the solute from the Data Table and its molar mass.

$$30.3 \text{ g} \times \frac{1 \text{ mole}}{58.45 \text{ g}} = 0.518 \text{ mole NaCl}$$

$$30.1 \text{ g} \times \frac{1 \text{ mole}}{342.31 \text{ g}} = 0.0879 \text{ mole } C_{12}H_{22}O_{11}$$

$$30.3 \text{ g} \times \frac{1 \text{ mole}}{147.02 \text{ g}} = 0.206 \text{ mole } CaCl_2$$

$$30.0 \text{ g} \times \frac{1 \text{ mole}}{241.43 \text{ g}} = 0.124 \text{ mole } AlCl_3$$

3. Calculate the experimental value of the freezing point depression, ΔT_f for each solute, using the equation below.

$$T_f \text{ (pure solvent)} - T_f \text{ (solution)} = \Delta T_f \text{ (in °C)}$$

   Example: $T_f(H_2O) - T_f(NaCl \text{ solution}) = 0.0 \text{ °C} - (-16.7 \text{ °C}) = 16.7 \text{ °C} = \Delta T_f$

4. Calculate the ΔT_f per mole of solute.

$$\Delta T_f/\text{mole} = \frac{16.7 \text{ °C}}{0.518 \text{ mole}} = 32.2 \text{ °C/mole NaCl}$$

Freezing Point Depression

Teacher's Notes

$$\Delta T_f/mole = \frac{1.5\ °C}{0.0879\ mole} = 17.1\ °C/mole\ C_{12}H_{22}O_{11}$$

$$\Delta T_f/mole = \frac{11.5\ °C}{0.206\ mole} = 55.8\ °C/mole\ CaCl_2$$

$$\Delta T_f/mole = \frac{11.1\ °C}{0.124\ mole} = 89.5\ °C/mole\ AlCl_3$$

5. For each solute that dissociates in water, write a balanced equation for its dissociation reaction. Determine the ideal value of i for each solute. This is the number of particles formed when one formula unit of the solute dissolves in water. *Note:* Waters of hydration are NOT included in the value of i.

$NaCl(s) \rightarrow Na^+(aq) + Cl^-(aq)$ $i = 2$

$C_{12}H_{22}O_{11}(s) \rightarrow C_{12}H_{22}O_{11}(aq)$ $i = 1$

$CaCl_2(s) \rightarrow Ca^{2+}(aq) + 2Cl^-(aq)$ $i = 3$

$AlCl_3(s) \rightarrow Al^{3+}(aq) + 3Cl^-(aq)$ $i = 4$

6. Calculate the concentration of each solution in molality, m, defined as the number of moles of solute per kilogram of solvent.

$$\text{Molality} = m = \frac{\text{moles of solute}}{\text{kilogram of solvent}}$$

$$\frac{0.518\ mole\ NaCl}{100.2\ g\ H_2O} \times \frac{1000\ g}{1\ kg} = 5.17\ m\ NaCl$$

$$\frac{0.0879\ mole\ C_{12}H_{22}O_{11}}{100.8\ g\ H_2O} \times \frac{1000\ g}{1\ kg} = 0.872\ m\ C_{12}H_{22}O_{11}$$

$$\frac{0.206\ mole\ CaCl_2}{100.7\ g\ H_2O} \times \frac{1000\ g}{1\ kg} = 2.05\ m\ CaCl_2$$

$$\frac{0.124\ mole\ AlCl_3}{100.1\ g\ H_2O} \times \frac{1000\ g}{1\ kg} = 1.24\ m\ AlCl_3$$

7. Calculate the theoretical value of the freezing point depression for each solute based on the molality of the solution (m) and the ideal number of solute particles (i). Use Equation 1 from the *Background* section, $K_f = 1.86\ °C/m$, and the calculated values for m and i.

$\Delta T_f\ (theor) = K_f \times m \times i$

$\Delta T_f\ (theor) = 1.86\ °C/m \times 5.17\ m \times 2 = 19.2\ °C$ for NaCl

$\Delta T_f\ (theor) = 1.86\ °C/m \times 0.872\ m \times 1 = 1.62\ °C$ for $C_{12}H_{22}O_{11}$

$\Delta T_f\ (theor) = 1.86\ °C/m \times 2.05\ m \times 3 = 11.4\ °C$ for $CaCl_2$

$\Delta T_f\ (theor) = 1.86\ °C/m \times 1.24\ m \times 4 = 9.23\ °C\ AlCl_3$

Flinn ChemTopic™ Labs — Solubility and Solutions

Teacher Notes

8. Compare the experimental and theoretical values of ΔT_f for each solute. Discuss possible sources of error in this experiment and their likely effect on the experimental ΔT_f values.

   Sucrose gave the best agreement with the theoretical ΔT_f value. It was the most dilute solution (in molality) and also the only nonelectrolyte in the study. (1) The ions or impurities in tap water and in the crushed ice may have affected the freezing point. To prevent this, distilled or deionized water could have been used to make the ice. (2) Solutes dissolve slower at low temperatures; temperature readings may have been taken before all of the solid was dissolved. (3) The measured T_f values are not true freezing points because the composition of the remaining liquid changes as part of the liquid freezes. Solutions do not have constant freezing points, as pure substances do.

9. Which solute had the greatest freezing point depression per mole? Which had the least? Is this what would be expected? Explain.

   Aluminum chloride had the greatest freezing point depression per mole and sucrose had the lowest. This is expected because each formula unit of aluminum chloride dissociates into four particles (ions) in solution while a sucrose molecule remains as one single particle when in solution. Freezing point depression is a colligative property that depends only on the number of particles or ions in solution.

10. Prepare a graph ΔT_f/mole on the y-axis versus i on the x-axis. Describe the relationship shown by the graph.

    The graph is approximately linear, suggesting a directly proportional relationship between i and ΔT_f/mole. Although the graph verifies the relationship expressed in Equation 1, it also shows that the real i-values differ from their theoretical or ideal values.

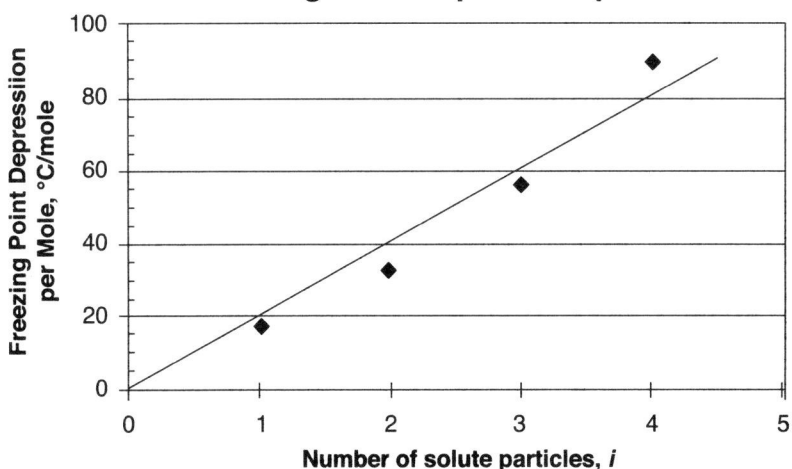

Effect of Number of Particles on the Freezing Point Depression per Mole

Freezing Point Depression

61   Freezing Point Depression

Teacher's Notes

Results Table *(Student results will vary.)*

Beaker Number	1	2	3	4
Solute	NaCl	$C_{12}H_{22}O_{11}$	$CaCl_2 \cdot 2H_2O$	$AlCl_3 \cdot 6H_2O$
Molar Mass (g/mole)	58.45	342.31	147.02	241.43
Moles of Solute	.518	.0879	.206	.124
ΔT_f (exp)	16.7	1.5	11.5	11.1
$\dfrac{\Delta T_f \text{ (exp)}}{\text{mole}}$	32.2	17.1	55.8	89.5
i (ideal value)	2	1	3	4
m	5.17	.872	2.05	1.24
ΔT_f (theor)	19.2	1.62	11.4	9.23

Demonstrations

Teacher Notes

Aloha Chemical Sunset
Colloids and Light Scattering

Introduction

Watch as the sun sets over a chemical reaction! The reaction of sodium thiosulfate with hydrochloric acid produces elemental sulfur, which precipitates from solution to form a colloidal mixture. When the reaction is carried out on an overhead projector, the light from the projector is scattered by the colloidal sulfur particles and produces a multicolored chemical sunset.

Concepts

- Colloid
- Light scattering
- Tyndall effect

Materials

Hydrochloric acid solution, 1 M, HCl, 8 mL

Sodium thiosulfate solution, 0.2 M, $Na_2S_2O_3$, 14 mL

Petri dish, 100 × 15 mm

Tropical sunset cutout

Graduated cylinder, 25-mL

Overhead projector

Paper

Scissors

Safety Precautions

Hydrochloric acid is moderately toxic by ingestion and inhalation and is corrosive to eyes and skin. Sodium thiosulfate solution is a body tissue irritant. The sulfur produced in this reaction has low toxicity but may be a skin and mucous membrane irritant. The smell of the sulfur may become irritating—transfer the Petri dish to the hood when the demonstration is over. The reaction also produces sulfur dioxide gas, which is a skin and eye irritant. Wear chemical splash goggles, chemical-resistant gloves, and a chemical-resistant apron. Please consult current Material Safety Data Sheets for additional safety information.

Procedure

1. Trace a circle the size of the Petri dish on a piece of opaque paper and cut out the circle to provide a "frame" for the chemical sunset (Figure 1a). Place this frame on the overhead projector.

2. Obtain a photocopy of the tropical sunset picture (page 64) and cut out along all of the outside edges to obtain a silhouette (Figure 1b).

3. Place the tropical sunset cutout inside its circular frame as shown in Figure 1c.

4. Place the Petri dish on the overhead projector and center the dish on top of the cutout.

5. Turn on the overhead projector and focus the tropical sunset picture on a projector screen or wall.

6. Measure 14 mL of 0.2 M sodium thiosulfate solution and pour it into the Petri dish.

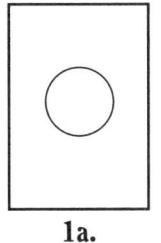

1a.   1b.   1c.

Figure 1.

Colloids may be classified based on the nature of the dispersed phase and the continuous phase. Familiar examples of colloids (and their dispersed/continuous phases) include milk (solid/liquid), aerosols (liquid/gas), and foams (gas/liquid or solid).

Aloha Chemical Sunset

Demonstrations

Teacher Notes

7. Measure 8 mL 1 M of hydrochloric acid solution and pour it into the Petri dish. Stir the mixture.

8. Observe the color of the projected light on the screen or wall. *(The color of the transmitted light will slowly change from red and orange to blue and green, and finally to dark gray.)*

Disposal

Please consult your current *Flinn Scientific Catalog/Reference Manual* for general guidelines and specific procedures governing the disposal of laboratory waste. The insoluble sulfur may be separated by filtration and disposed of in a landfill according to Flinn Suggested Disposal Method #26a. The remaining filtrate may be disposed of down the drain with plenty of excess water according to Flinn Suggested Disposal Method #26b.

Tips

- Experiment with the volumes of reagents used and the rate at which hydrochloric acid is added to produce different special effects in the chemical sunset.

- Add flair to the presentation by playing Hawaiian music in the background as the demonstration is silently presented to the students.

Discussion

Reaction of sodium thiosulfate with hydrochloric acid produces elemental sulfur, according to the following overall reaction equation.

$$Na_2S_2O_3(aq) + 2HCl(aq) \rightarrow S(s) + SO_2(aq) + H_2O(l) + 2NaCl$$

Elemental sulfur precipitates rapidly from solution but the solid remains dispersed throughout the aqueous phase. The solid sulfur forms a sol, a colloidal mixture that may appear uniform throughout (colloids often look milky or cloudy). In contrast to the uniformly dispersed particles in a true solution, however, the dispersed particles in a colloid are relatively large and thus will scatter light that is passed through the mixture. The scattering of light by a colloid—called the Tyndall effect—makes it possible to view a beam of light as it passes through the mixture. As the colloidal sulfur particles grow, the light from the overhead projector is scattered. The changing colors of the sunset are produced because different wavelengths of visible light are scattered to different degrees. The shorter wavelengths of light (blue and green) are scattered more than the longer wavelengths (red and orange). The longer wavelengths of light pass through the mixture and produce a red-orange color in the projected (transmitted) light. As the amount and particle size of the colloidal sulfur increases, the wavelength dependence of the amount of light scattering diminishes and other colors are seen. Eventually the mixture becomes opaque and no light passes through—night falls and the sunset fades to black!

The chemical sunset illustrates the process involved in a true sunset as well. Dust particles in the atmosphere scatter the light from the sun. When the sun is near the horizon and the scattered light is viewed directly (rather than from an angle), the light appears orange or pink.

Flinn ChemTopic™ Labs — Solubility and Solutions

Teacher Notes

Solutions, Colloids, and Suspensions
Principles and Properties

Introduction

Solutions, colloids, and suspensions are mixtures in which one substance appears to be more or less uniformly dispersed throughout another substance. The size of the dispersed particles influences the properties of a mixture and determines whether the mixture is a solution, colloid or suspension. Are the particles large enough that they will settle upon standing or be trapped by a filter? Are the particles small enough that they will pass through a semipermeable membrane?

Concepts

- Solution
- Colloid
- Light scattering
- Semipermeable membrane

Materials

Ammonium hydroxide solution, 6 M, NH_4OH, 1 mL
Copper(II) sulfate solution, 0.1 M, $CuSO_4$, 100 mL
Colloidal starch, 0.5%, 130 mL*
Hydrochloric acid solution, 1 M, HCl, 25 mL
Iodine–Potassium iodide test solution for starch, 12 mL
Sodium thiosulfate solution, 0.2 M, $Na_2S_2O_3$, 400 mL
Starch suspension, 1%, 100 mL*
Beakers, 600-mL, 2
Distilled water, 300 mL

Dialysis tubing, 25-mm wide, 4–6"
Dialysis tubing clamps or string to tie tubing
Erlenmeyer flasks, 125-mL, 6
Filter funnels, 3
Filter paper, qualitative, 3
Funnel support clamp and ring stand
Pipets, Beral-type, 3
Stoppers to fit Erlenmeyer flasks, 3

*See the *Tips* section for instructions on how to prepare colloidal starch and a starch suspension.

Safety Precautions

Ammonium hydroxide solution is a corrosive liquid and is extremely irritating to the eyes and respiratory tract. It is toxic by ingestion and inhalation. Work with ammonium hydroxide in the hood or in a well-ventilated lab only. Hydrochloric acid is moderately toxic by ingestion and inhalation and is corrosive to eyes and skin. Copper(II) sulfate solution is a body tissue irritant and is slightly toxic by ingestion. Sodium thiosulfate solution is a body tissue irritant. Iodine–potassium iodide solution is a skin and eye irritant. Wear chemical splash goggles, chemical-resistant gloves, and a chemical-resistant apron. Please consult current Material Safety Data Sheets for additional safety information.

Demonstrations

Procedure

Teacher Notes

1. Obtain 100 mL of copper(II) sulfate solution, colloidal starch, and starch suspension in three separate 125-mL Erlenmeyer flasks.

Part A. Are the particles large enough to settle upon standing?

2. Stopper the Erlenmeyer flasks and shake each mixture vigorously for 15 sec. Allow the mixtures to stand for a few minutes and observe. *(Upon standing, a white solid slowly settles out of the starch suspension. The copper sulfate solution and colloidal starch do not settle upon standing.)*

Part B. Are the particles small enough to pass through a filter?

3. Set up three filter funnels with qualitative filter paper and place the funnels in a funnel support clamp.

4. Briefly shake each mixture from step 2 and pour half of each mixture through a separate funnel. Collect the filtrates in clean, 125-mL Erlenmeyer flasks or large test tubes.

5. Observe whether any solid remains behind on the filter paper in each case. *(The copper sulfate solution and colloidal starch pass untouched through the filter paper and the filtrates look identical to the starting solutions. The starch suspension separates into a white solid, which remains behind on the filter paper, and a clear and colorless filtrate.)*

6. Add 10 drops of 6 M ammonium hydroxide solution to the original copper sulfate solution and to the filtrate. Did the composition of the solution change? *(No change—both the original solution and the filtrate turn a deep, royal blue color due to the formation of a copper–ammonia complex ion.)*

7. Add 10 drops of iodine test solution to the original colloidal starch and to the filtrate. Did the composition of the mixture change? *(No change—both the original mixture and the filtrate turn dark blue due to the formation of the familiar iodine–starch complex.)*

8. Add 10 drops of iodine test solution to the original starch suspension and to the filtrate. Did the composition of the suspension change? *(The original starch suspension turns dark blue. The filtrate turns pale, greenish-brown.)*

Part C. Are the particles small enough to pass through a semipermeable membrane?

9. Obtain a six-inch piece of pre-soaked dialysis tubing and clamp or tie off one end with a piece of string. *Note:* See the *Tips* section for directions for soaking the dialysis tubing.

10. Pour about 30 mL of colloidal starch into the dialysis tubing. Clamp or tie off the other end of the tubing so that the tube is securely tied and will not leak.

11. Add about 300 mL of distilled or deionized water, followed by 10 mL of iodine test solution, to a 600-mL beaker.

Part C demonstrates that solute particles (I_2 and KI) pass through the membrane, but that colloidal particles (starch) do not. If desired, a second dialysis demonstration may be done using the $CuSO_4$ solution (in the bag). Copper and sulfate ions will diffuse through the membrane and the water in the beaker will turn blue.

Flinn ChemTopic™ Labs — Solubility and Solutions

Demonstrations

Teacher Notes

12. Place the dialysis tubing in the beaker and observe and explain any color changes in the beaker and in the dialysis tubing. *(The colloidal starch solution turns blue within a few minutes. No color change is observed in the iodine solution in the beaker. Iodine molecules are small enough to pass through the semipermeable dialysis membrane. Starch molecules are too large and do not pass through the membrane.)*

Part D. Are the particles large enough to scatter light?

13. Obtain 400 mL of 0.2 M sodium thiosulfate solution in a large, 600-mL beaker.

14. Shine a flashlight through the solution in the beaker and observe. *(The beam of light passes through the solution and can be projected on a screen or wall. The path of light in the solution itself is not visible when viewed through the side of the beaker.)*

15. Add about 25 mL of 1 M hydrochloric acid to the sodium thiosulfate solution and shine a flashlight through the resulting mixture.

16. Observe and explain any changes in the path of the beam of light. *(In a few minutes the mixture will become turbid due to the formation of colloidal sulfur. As the turbidity increases, the beam of light becomes visible as it passes through the mixture. The beam of light becomes visible due to light scattering by the relatively large colloidal sulfur particles. Because blue light is scattered more than red light, the reflected light in the mixture itself appears blue while the transmitted light that emerges from the mixture appears dark orange.)*

Disposal

Please consult your current *Flinn Scientific Catalog/Reference Manual* for general guidelines and specific procedures governing the disposal of laboratory waste. Any remaining copper sulfate solutions and starch solution may be disposed of down the drain with plenty of excess water according to Flinn Suggested Disposal Method #26b. Excess iodine–potassium iodide solution may be reduced with 50% sodium thiosulfate solution and disposed of according to Flinn Suggested Disposal Method #12a. The sulfur produced in the light scattering test may be separated by filtration and disposed of in a landfill according to Flinn Suggested Disposal Method #26a.

Tips

- To prepare 0.5% colloidal starch, make a paste of 0.5 g of soluble starch with a small amount of water and add the paste to 100 mL of boiling water. Stir the mixture until it appears homogeneous, and allow the colloidal starch to slowly cool to room temperature before using. Ready-made 0.5% colloidal starch "solution" is available from Flinn Scientific (Catalog No. S0151) and may also be used.

- To prepare 1% starch suspension, add 1 g of soluble starch to 100 mL of water and stir to mix.

- Dialysis tubing is a semipermeable membrane made of cellulose. Small molecules pass through the membrane, while larger molecules do not. The tubing must be soaked in water before use—rinse the tubing with distilled or deionized water and allow it to soak for 5–10 minutes prior to use. Once wet, the tubing should not be allowed to dry out again.

Instead of, or in addition to Part D, do the "Aloha Chemical Sunset" demonstration in this book (pp 63–64).

Solutions, Colloids, and Suspensions

Demonstrations

Teacher Notes

Discussion

Solutions, colloids, and suspensions differ from one another in the size of the particles that are dispersed throughout a continuous phase. They are defined and distinguished from one another primarily in terms of their properties. Colloids, for example, may be defined as mixtures in which the dispersed particles are small enough to pass through a filter but too large to pass through a semipermeable membrane. Although colloids, like solutions, may appear uniform throughout, only solutions are considered truly homogeneous mixtures. The particles in a colloid are large enough that they will reflect or scatter light in all directions. In a true solution the dispersed particles are too small to scatter visible light. Suspensions are defined as mixtures in which the particles are large enough that they will settle upon standing (due to the effect of gravity) and will not pass through a filter. The following table summarizes the properties of solutions, colloids, and suspensions. Notice that the particle size for each type of mixture is a range and not an absolute or fixed value. There is thus a continuum of properties for solutions, colloids, and suspensions.

Property	Solution	Colloid	Suspension
Particle Size	0.1–1 nm (atoms, ions, and small molecules)	1–200 nm (large protein molecules)	>200 nm (aggregates of large molecules)
Light Scattering	None	Tyndall effect	Tyndall effect
Settling Behavior	Stable, does not separate.	Stable, does not separate	Particles separate on standing.
Filtration	Particles pass through filter.	Particles pass through filter.	Particles do not pass through filter.
Dialysis	Particles pass through membrane.	Particles do not pass through membrane.	Particles do not pass through membrane.

The scattering of light by particles in a mixture is called the Tyndall effect and makes it possible to view a beam of light as it passes through a colloid or a suspension. Different wavelengths of visible light are scattered to different degrees by the dispersed particles and so the light may appear different colors when viewed from the side or after it has passed through the mixture. In Part D, colloidal sulfur is produced by the reaction of sodium thiosulfate with hydrochloric acid (Equation 1). Elemental (solid) sulfur forms rapidly but remains dispersed throughout the aqueous phase. The dispersed sulfur particles are relatively large and will thus scatter or reflect light that is passed through the mixture.

$$Na_2S_2O_3(aq) + 2HCl(aq) \rightarrow S(s) + SO_2(aq) + H_2O(l) + 2NaCl \qquad \textit{Equation 1}$$

Flinn ChemTopic™ Labs — Solubility and Solutions

Demonstrations

Teacher Notes

Alka-Seltzer® and Gas Solubility
Effect of Temperature

Introduction

Our understanding of chemical principles is shaped to a large extent by applications that we encounter in our daily lives. In the case of the effect of temperature on solubility, for example, students may draw on their everyday experiences preparing food and beverages and generalize that the solubility of a solute will increase with increasing temperature. In the case of solids and liquids, this generalization is usually true—the solubility of many solid and liquid solutes increases as the temperature increases. In the case of gases, however, this generalization is always wrong! Let's see what an Alka-Seltzer® tablet can teach us about the effect of temperature on the solubility of a gas.

Concepts

- Gas solubility
- Reversible reactions
- Thermal pollution

Materials

Alka-Seltzer® tablet

Bromthymol blue indicator solution, 0.04% aqueous, 10 mL

Sodium hydroxide solution, 1 M, NaOH, 5 mL

Tap water

Ice bath

Thermometer

Weighing paper or weighing dishes, 2

Balance

Beakers, 250-mL, 3

Beral-type pipets, thin stem, 2

Graduated cylinders, 10- and 25-mL, 1 each

Hot plate

Test tubes, extra large, 25 × 150 mm, 3 (or small beakers)

Test tube rack

Stirring rod

Safety Precautions

Sodium hydroxide solution is a corrosive liquid; it is especially dangerous to eyes and may burn skin. Wear chemical splash goggles, chemical-resistant gloves, and a chemical-resistant apron. Please consult current Material Safety Data Sheets for additional safety information.

Procedure

1. Add 200 mL of water to each of three 250-mL beakers. Place one beaker in an ice bath, heat the second beaker on a hot plate, and allow the third beaker to equilibrate at room temperature. *Note:* The room temperature beaker will serve as the experimental control for the amount of carbon dioxide gas dissolved in water at room temperature.

2. Obtain two 1.0-gram samples of Alka-Seltzer by snapping off pieces of the tablet and weighing them on weighing paper or in a weighing dish.

3. When the water on the hot plate has reached a temperature of 75–80 °C, remove it from the heat. Remove the cold water beaker from the ice bath at this time also.

Demonstrations

4. Using a graduated cylinder, add 3 mL of bromthymol blue indicator to each beaker, including the room temperature control. *(The water in each beaker should be blue-green, indicating a neutral pH.)*

5. Simultaneously drop the two 1.0-gram samples of Alka-Seltzer into the hot and cold beakers. Carefully observe and compare all evidence of physical and chemical changes in each beaker. *(The Alka-Seltzer tablets will dissolve and effervesce in the water, producing carbon dioxide gas. The reaction occurs significantly faster in hot water than in cold water. The cold water reaction takes about 5 minutes, while the hot water reaction appears to be complete in about 30 seconds.)*

6. When the Alka-Seltzer tablets have fully dissolved, note the color and appearance of the solution in each beaker. *(The cold water reaction mixture is bright yellow; the hot water reaction mixture is lime green.)*

7. Measure the temperature of each solution, including the room temperature control, and label three large test tubes with the corresponding temperature.

8. Using a graduated cylinder, remove a 25-mL sample from each beaker, including the room temperature control, and place the sample in the appropriate labeled test tube.

9. Using a thin stem pipet, add 1 M sodium hydroxide solution dropwise to the cold water reaction mixture. Count the number of drops of NaOH that must be added to match the color of the room temperature control solution. Stir or swirl the solution between drops to ensure thorough mixing. *(For a cold water reaction mixture at 5 °C, six drops of NaOH are required to neutralize the excess dissolved carbon dioxide.)*

10. Repeat step 9 using the hot water reaction mixture, again comparing the color with that of the room temperature control. *(Only one drop of NaOH is required to neutralize the dissolved carbon dioxide.)*

11. *(Optional)* Obtain 400 mL of ice-cold (0–5 °C) water in a 600-mL beaker and add 2.0 g of Alka-Seltzer. Allow the tablet to dissolve completely, then withdraw a 25-mL sample and neutralize as described in step 9. Begin slowly heating the ice-cold reaction mixture on a hot plate. When the temperature is about 25 °C, withdraw a second 25-mL sample and titrate as before. Continue heating and analyzing samples at about 50 °C and 75 °C. Compare the number of drops of NaOH required to neutralize the dissolved carbon dioxide at each temperature. *[The number of drops of sodium hydroxide required to neutralize the dissolved carbon dioxide decreases in the following order: 6 drops (3 °C), 5 drops (25 °C), 4 drops (49 °C), and 3 drops (79 °C).]*

Disposal

Please consult your current *Flinn Scientific Catalog/Reference Manual* for general guidelines and specific procedures governing the disposal of laboratory waste. The final solutions may be disposed of down the drain with plenty of excess water according to Flinn Suggested Disposal Method #26b.

Demonstrations

Teacher Notes

Tips

- Bromthymol blue indicator is yellow when the pH is less than 6.0, blue when the pH is greater than 7.6, and various shades of green when the pH is between 6.0 and 7.6. Check the color of the tap water in each beaker before adding Alka-Seltzer in step 2. If the water is not blue or blue-green, add *one* drop of sodium hydroxide solution to each beaker.

- Other indicators that may be used in this demonstration include phenol red (transition range pH 6.8–8.4) and neutral red (transition range pH 6.8–8.0).

- Tap water is preferred over distilled or deionized water in this demonstration. The amount of dissolved carbon dioxide present naturally in water due to the carbon dioxide in air depends on the amount of dissolved bicarbonate. (The solubility of carbon dioxide decreases as the amount of dissolved bicarbonate increases.) Distilled or deionized water acts like a sponge in absorbing carbon dioxide from the air!

- The solubility of carbon dioxide at different temperatures may also be illustrated using a bottle of seltzer water. Remove the label and chill a 10-oz, clear-glass bottle of seltzer in an ice bath for 5 minutes. Open the bottle and quickly pour out ⅓ of the seltzer, add 1 mL of bromcresol green indicator solution (pH range 3.8–5.4), and immediately recap the bottle. *(The seltzer will be yellow, indicating a pH < 3.8.)* Allow the seltzer to warm to room temperature. Shake the bottle and vent, shake the bottle and vent—repeat this process until little excess pressure is released when the bottle is vented. *(The seltzer should be green at this point, indicating that less carbon dioxide is dissolved at room temperature than at 0 °C.)* Remove the cap from the bottle and place the bottle in a hot water bath at 80–90 °C. Observe the "outgassing" of carbon dioxide from the seltzer water as the solution is heated. *(The color of the solution changes to blue-green as the amount of dissolved carbon dioxide decreases at the higher temperature.)*

Discussion

Alka-Seltzer tablets contain aspirin, sodium bicarbonate, and citric acid The active antacid or buffering ingredients are sodium bicarbonate, a weak base, and citric acid, a weak acid. Citric acid is a triprotic acid (three ionizable hydrogens). When the tablet dissolves in water, one mole of citric acid reacts with three moles of bicarbonate ion. The products of the neutralization reaction are citrate ion, carbon dioxide ("plop-plop-fizz-fizz") and water (Equation 1). The citrate ion acts as a buffer against "excess stomach acid."

$$H_3C_6H_5O_7(aq) + 3HCO_3^-(aq) \rightarrow C_6H_5O_7^{3-}(aq) + 3CO_2(g) + 3H_2O(l) \qquad \textit{Equation 1}$$

When carbon dioxide dissolves in water (Equation 2), it combines reversibly with water to form carbonic acid (Equation 3), which behaves as a weak acid (Equation 4).

$$CO_2(g) \rightleftharpoons CO_2(aq) \qquad \textit{Equation 2}$$

$$CO_2(aq) + H_2O(l) \rightleftharpoons H_2CO_3(aq) \qquad \textit{Equation 3}$$

$$H_2CO_3(aq) + H_2O(l) \rightleftharpoons HCO_3^-(aq) + H_3O^+(aq) \qquad \textit{Equation 4}$$

Demonstrations

Notice that all three reactions (Equations 2–4) are reversible. In the case of Equations 3 and 4, the equilibria for these reactions strongly favor reactants rather than products. The overall result, however, is that carbon dioxide dissolves in water to give a weakly acidic solution (pH 3–5), and the acidity of the solution depends on the amount of dissolved carbon dioxide. Any factor, therefore, that influences the solubility of carbon dioxide gas in water will also affect the pH of the solution and the total amount of acid present. In this demonstration, the effect of temperature on the solubility of carbon dioxide can be followed by observing both the indicator color changes and the "neutralization equivalent" of the solution (number of drops of NaOH required to neutralize a given volume of solution). The cold Alka-Seltzer solution is yellow (pH < 6.0) and requires six drops of NaOH per 25 mL of solution. The hot Alka-Seltzer solution is green (pH = ca. 6.8) and requires only one drop of NaOH per 25 mL of solution. Both of these results clearly reveal that the solubility of carbon dioxide decreases as the temperature increases.

The effect of temperature on gas solubility has important implications in biology and in the chemistry of the environment. Artificial thermal pollution of lakes and streams occurs when power plants or other industrial plants discharge cooling water back into the natural water source at a higher temperature than it was originally. The amount of dissolved oxygen present in thermally polluted lakes and streams decreases at the higher temperatures, which reduces in turn the amount of oxygen available for aquatic organisms. The reduced oxygen availability (coupled with increased biological oxygen demand at higher temperatures) can have serious consequences for the number and type of organisms that live in the water.

Teacher Notes

Demonstrations

Teacher Notes

Sorting Out Solutions
Hydrogen Bonding Demonstration

Introduction

Two clear liquids are combined to form a homogeneous solution. As a solid is added, the solution begins to separate into two layers. As more solid is added, the two layers become more distinct.

Concepts

- Miscible liquids
- Hydrogen bonding
- Salting-out

Materials

Ethyl alcohol, 95%, 150 mL

Glycerol, 50 mL

Potassium carbonate, K_2CO_3, 85 g

Water, distilled or deionized, and wash bottle

Beaker, 600-mL

Food coloring (optional)

Magnetic stirrer and stirring bar

Volumetric flask, 100-mL (with stopper)

Safety Precautions

Ethyl alcohol is flammable, a dangerous fire risk, and toxic by ingestion and inhalation. Keep away from sources of heat and flame. Potassium carbonate is a body tissue irritant and is slightly toxic by ingestion. Glycerol is also a skin and eye irritant and a possible allergen. Wear chemical splash goggles, chemical-resistant gloves, and a chemical-resistant apron. Please consult current Material Safety Data Sheets for additional safety information.

Procedure

Part A. Volume Contraction Due to Hydrogen Bonding

1. Add approximately 50 mL of glycerol to the 100-mL volumetric flask.

2. Using a wash bottle, float water on top of the glycerol in the flask, adding water just to the 100-mL mark on the neck of the flask. Show students that the flask is filled to the mark.

3. Insert a stopper into the flask and invert the flask several times to mix the contents.

4. Show students that the flask now contains less than 100 mL of liquid. The decrease in volume of approximately 4 mL is due to the strong attractive forces between the glycerol and water molecules.

5. The formation of the hydrogen bonds is exothermic. Allow student volunteers to feel the sides of the flask—students will notice that the solution feels warm.

Part B. Separation of Solutions

6. Add 150 mL of ethyl alcohol, followed by 150 mL of distilled or deionized water, to a 600-mL beaker.

7. Place a magnetic stirring bar in the beaker and place the beaker on the magnetic stirrer. Mix the solution until it is homogeneous. Add food coloring if desired (see *Tips*).

Add different food colors to the mixture in Part B and see what happens to the layers. Yellow is the only dye that is soluble in the organic and aqueous layers. Blue, red and green dyes (except the yellow portion) show a greater affinity for the organic layer.

Sorting Out Solutions

Demonstrations

8. Add 25 g of potassium carbonate to the solution and stir until all the solid has dissolved. Two separate layers will begin to appear. The top layer is the larger volume and is the organic mixture. The smaller, bottom layer is the aqueous mixture.

9. Continue to add potassium carbonate in 20-g portions. The two liquid layers will become equal in volume after approximately 85 g of potassium carbonate has been added.

Teacher Notes

Disposal

Please consult your current *Flinn Scientific Catalog/Reference Manual* for general guidelines and specific procedures governing the disposal of laboratory waste. The final solutions may be flushed down the drain with excess water according to Flinn Suggested Disposal Method #26b.

Tip

- Use food coloring to enhance the visual effect of the demonstration in Part B. Add a few drops of blue and a few drops of yellow dyes to the ethyl alcohol and water solution to give it a green color. As the solution separates, the upper layer will remain green but the lower layer will turn yellow. If just green food coloring is used, the solution will "sort out" into a dark green upper layer and a light green lower layer.

Discussion

In Part A, the volume contraction upon mixing glycerol and water shows that hydrogen bonding is a strong intermolecular force. It is so strong between glycerol (with three —OH groups) and water molecules that the volume of the solution is actually 4% less than the combined volume of the individual pure liquids. As in any bond formation process, energy is released to the surroundings when the hydrogen bonds form.

Water and ethyl alcohol are miscible liquids that are held together by strong hydrogen bonding. It is extremely difficult to separate this mixture—distillation even gives an azeotrope, a constant-boiling mixture consisting of 5% water and 95% ethyl alcohol. When potassium carbonate is added to the solution, the potassium and carbonate ions dissociate and are hydrated. The ions attract the water molecules and disrupt the hydrogen bonds binding the water and ethyl alcohol molecules. As the layers form, the ethyl alcohol/water mixture will appear on top of the more dense aqueous potassium carbonate solution. As more potassium carbonate is added, more water will be removed from the ethyl alcohol/water mixture. The phenomenon is known as *salting-out* and is widely used to separate and purify organic compounds from aqueous mixtures. It is also used to precipitate proteins from aqueous cell extracts.

After adding 85 g of potassium carbonate, the two liquid layers will be approximately equal in volume and all water will be removed from the organic layer. Any additional potassium carbonate added will dissolve in the aqueous layer until it reaches saturation.

The dyes used in food coloring are large organic molecules with charged or polar end groups. The charged ends allow the dye molecules to dissolve in water as well as organic solvents. When potassium carbonate is added, the water molecules are so attracted to the potassium and carbonate ions that no water molecules are available to hydrate the larger organic dyes. The organic dyes thus remain behind in the organic layer. Only the yellow dye will dissolve in both the ethyl alcohol layer and the potassium carbonate solution layer.

Flinn ChemTopic™ Labs — Solubility and Solutions

Demonstrations

Teacher Notes

Instant Hand Warmers
Supersaturated and Saturated Solutions

Introduction

Heat is often required to dissolve crystals and form a saturated solution. What happens when a supersaturated solution is allowed to crystallize?

Concepts

- Saturated solution
- Supersaturated solution
- Crystallization
- Exothermic reaction

Materials

Sodium acetate trihydrate, $NaC_2H_3O_2 \cdot 3H_2O$, 160 g

Sodium chloride (optional), 3–5 crystals

Water, distilled or deionized

The Heat Solution™ Instant Hand Warmer

Erlenmeyer flask, 500-mL

Graduated cylinder, 100-mL

Stirring rod

Balance

Beaker, 600-mL

Hot plate

Heat-resistant gloves

Thermometer (optional)

Petri dish

Tongs

Safety Precautions

Sodium acetate is slightly toxic by ingestion, inhalation, and skin absorption and is a body-tissue irritant. The crystallization reaction is quite exothermic—wear heat-resistant gloves when handling the hot flask. Wear chemical splash goggles, chemical-resistant gloves, and a chemical-resistant apron. Please consult current Material Safety Data Sheets for additional safety information.

Preparation

Prepare a supersaturated solution of sodium acetate by dissolving 160 g of sodium acetate trihydrate in 30–40 mL of distilled or deionized water in a 500-mL Erlenmeyer flask. Heat the mixture on a hot plate, stirring occasionally, until all the solid has dissolved. Wash down the sides of the flask with a small amount of distilled water from a wash bottle to dissolve any crystals. Remove the flask from the heat, cover it with a small beaker or Parafilm™, and allow the solution to cool undisturbed until ready for use. For best results, use new and clean glassware that is not scratched. Practice preparing the supersaturated solution before attempting this demonstration.

For an interesting crystallization effect, add the supersaturated solution from a buret onto the seed crystals. A stalagmite will grow upward from the Petri dish and may eventually reach the tip of the buret.

Procedure

1. Place a few crystals of sodium acetate trihydrate in a Petri dish and slowly pour the supersaturated solution onto the crystals. *(Crystallization from the supersaturated solution will occur immediately, forming a mound of solid, milky-white sodium acetate. The solid will feel noticeably warm to the touch.)*

Instand Hand Warmers

Demonstrations

2. Change the shape of the mound or form pillars of different shapes and heights by slowly pouring the solution in different locations in the Petri dish.

3. *(Optional)* Place a few crystals of sodium chloride in a Petri dish and pour the supersaturated sodium acetate solution onto it. *(Crystallization does not take place. In order for a solid to act as a "seed crystal," its crystal structure must be similar to that of the supersaturated solute in solution.)*

4. Obtain a Heat Solution Instant Hand Warmer and observe its contents—the pouch, liquid, and metal disk. Discuss the evidence for whether the solution is saturated, unsaturated or supersaturated. *(Based on observation, the hand warmer is initially **not** a saturated solution, because no crystals can be seen.)*

5. Follow the directions on the hand warmer to activate it. Pass around the hand warmer to observe what it looks and feels like. *(Flexing the metal disk back and forth causes the solution to crystallize instantly. There is no liquid left in the pouch and the pouch feels very hot to the touch. The hand warmer will remain hot for about 30 minutes.)*

6. Is the activated solution saturated, unsaturated or supersaturated? *(The solution is saturated, because crystals can be seen.)*

7. At room temperature, the initial solution in the hand warmer (before activation) must have been supersaturated. Discuss why crystallization of the supersaturated solution is an exothermic reaction. *(Watching a solution crystallize or "freeze" and get hot at the same time will surely seem counter-intuitive to your students. Turn it around, however, and it makes sense. Since melting is an endothermic process that absorbs heat from the surroundings, freezing must be an exothermic process that releases heat to the surroundings.)*

8. Place the activated hand warmer in a boiling water bath in a beaker on the hot plate to redissolve the crystals. Remove the pouch from the boiling water with tongs and allow it to cool undisturbed. The pouch may be reused about 30–40 times before it must be discarded.

Disposal

Please consult your current *Flinn Scientific Catalog/Reference Manual* for general guidelines and specific procedures governing the disposal of laboratory waste. The supersaturated solution of sodium acetate may be saved for future use. The instant hand warmer may be regenerated and reused about 30–40 times before disposing of it in the trash according to Flinn Suggested Disposal Method #26b.

Tip

- Sodium thiosulfate pentahydrate (hypo) readily forms supersaturated solutions and may also be used in the first part of this demonstration (steps 1–3) to demonstrate crystallization from a supersaturated solution.

Teacher Notes

To demonstrate the heat effect in crystallization of the supersaturated solution, place a digital thermometer with an extension probe (Flinn Catalog No. AP8559) in the Erlenmeyer flask. Add a seed crystal and watch as the solution temperature increases and the solution "freezes"!

Demonstrations

Teacher Notes

Discussion

The Heat Solution™ contains a supersaturated, supercooled solution of sodium acetate and a stainless steel disk in a sealed vinyl pouch. When the metal disk is bent, it causes a single crystal of sodium acetate trihydrate to crystallize and act as a seed crystal. The seed crystal essentially starts a chain reaction that causes the entire solution to crystallize. The liquid becomes a solid and releases so much heat that it "freezes"!

The unactivated instant hand warmer solution is both supersaturated and supercooled, since it contains more dissolved sodium acetate than a saturated solution and has been cooled to below its freezing point without crystallization occurring. In a sealed container, the solution may be cooled to as low as –10 °C without freezing. When the crystallization is activated, the temperature of the solution increases to the freezing (melting) point of sodium acetate trihydrate, which is about 58 °C. At this temperature, the sodium acetate solution changes from a liquid to a solid. The pouch will not exceed this temperature when activated because as additional heat is released in the crystallization process, it is used to melt the crystals that have previously formed. The temperature of the system, therefore, will not rise above the freezing (melting) point until all the solid has melted again! Since the temperature of the system is above room temperature and heat is continuously lost to the surroundings, eventually all the sodium acetate trihydrate will solidify rather than melt.

The instant hand warmer may be regenerated for repeat use by heating the solidified crystals above 58 °C, whereupon the sodium acetate trihydrate crystals will melt. (Alternatively, the sodium acetate trihydrate crystals may be said to dissolve in their own water of hydration.) The reversible crystallization–dissolving process for sodium acetate trihydrate may be represented by means of the following equation.

$$NaC_2H_3O_2 \cdot 3H_2O(l) \rightleftharpoons NaC_2H_3O_2 \cdot 3H_2O(s) + \text{heat (19.7 kJ/mole)}$$

The forward reaction represents crystallization (freezing). Notice that heat is released in this reaction—the reaction is exothermic, as evidenced by the fact that the activated pouch becomes very warm and fulfills its intended application. The reverse reaction represents the dissolving or melting process. Notice that heat must be added to the system in this direction.

Instand Hand Warmers

Safety and Disposal

Safety and Disposal Guidelines

Safety Guidelines

Teachers owe their students a duty of care to protect them from harm and to take reasonable precautions to prevent accidents from occurring. A teacher's duty of care includes the following:

- Supervising students in the classroom.
- Providing adequate instructions for students to perform the tasks required of them.
- Warning students of the possible dangers involved in performing the activity.
- Providing safe facilities and equipment for the performance of the activity.
- Maintaining laboratory equipment in proper working order.

Safety Contract

The first step in creating a safe laboratory environment is to develop a safety contract that describes the rules of the laboratory for your students. Before a student ever sets foot in a laboratory, the safety contract should be reviewed and then signed by the student and a parent or guardian. Please contact Flinn Scientific at 800-452-1261 or visit the Flinn Website at www.flinnsci.com to request a free copy of the Flinn Scientific Safety Contract.

To fulfill your duty of care, observe the following guidelines:

1. **Be prepared.** Practice all experiments and demonstrations beforehand. Never perform a lab activity if you have not tested it, if you do not understand it, or if you do not have the resources to perform it safely.

2. **Set a good example.** The teacher is the most visible and important role model. Wear your safety goggles whenever you are working in the lab, even (or especially) when class is not in session. Students learn from your good example—whether you are preparing reagents, testing a procedure, or performing a demonstration.

3. **Maintain a safe lab environment.** Provide high-quality goggles that offer adequate protection and are comfortable to wear. Make sure there is proper safety equipment in the laboratory and that it is maintained in good working order. Inspect all safety equipment on a regular basis to ensure its readiness.

4. **Start with safety.** Incorporate safety into each laboratory exercise. Begin each lab period with a discussion of the properties of the chemicals or procedures used in the experiment and any special precautions—including goggle use—that must be observed. Pre-lab assignments are an ideal mechanism to ensure that students are prepared for lab and understand the safety precautions. Record all safety instruction in your lesson plan.

5. **Proper instruction.** Demonstrate new or unusual laboratory procedures before every activity. Instruct students on the safe way to handle chemicals, glassware, and equipment.

Safety and Disposal

6. **Supervision.** Never leave students unattended—always provide adequate supervision. Work with school administrators to make sure that class size does not exceed the capacity of the room or your ability to maintain a safe lab environment. Be prepared and alert to what students are doing so that you can prevent accidents before they happen.

7. **Understand your resources.** Know yourself, your students, and your resources. Use discretion in choosing experiments and demonstrations that match your background and fit within the knowledge and skill level of your students and the resources of your classroom. You are the best judge of what will work or not. Do not perform any activities that you feel are unsafe, that you are uncomfortable performing, or that you do not have the proper equipment for.

Safety Precautions

Specific safety precautions have been written for every experiment and demonstration in this book. The safety information describes the hazardous nature of each chemical and the specific precautions that must be followed to avoid exposure or accidents. The safety section also alerts you to potential dangers in the procedure or techniques. Regardless of what lab program you use, it is important to maintain a library of current Material Safety Data Sheets for all chemicals in your inventory. Please consult current MSDS for additional safety, handling, and disposal information.

Disposal Procedures

The disposal procedures included in this book are based on the Suggested Laboratory Chemical Disposal Procedures found in the *Flinn Scientific Catalog/Reference Manual*. The disposal procedures are only suggestions—do not use these procedures without first consulting with your local government regulatory officials.

Many of the experiments and demonstrations produce small volumes of aqueous solutions that can be flushed down the drain with excess water. Do not use this procedure if your drains empty into groundwater through a septic system or into a storm sewer. Local regulations may be more strict on drain disposal than the practices suggested in this book and in the *Flinn Scientific Catalog/Reference Manual*. You must determine what types of disposal procedures are permitted in your area—contact your local authorities.

Any suggested disposal method that includes "discard in the trash" requires your active attention and involvement. Make sure that the material is no longer reactive, is placed in a suitable container (plastic bag or bottle), and is in accordance with local landfill regulations. Please do not inadvertently perform any extra "demonstrations" due to unpredictable chemical reactions occurring in your trash can. Think before you throw!

Finally, please read all the narratives before you attempt any Suggested Laboratory Chemical Disposal Procedure found in your current *Flinn Scientific Catalog/Reference Manual*.

Flinn Scientific is your most trusted and reliable source of reference, safety, and disposal information for all chemicals used in the high school science lab. To request a complimentary copy of the most recent *Flinn Scientific Catalog/Reference Manual,* call us at 800-452-1261 or visit our Web site at www.flinnsci.com.

National Science Education Standards

Experiments and Demonstrations

Content Standards	Factors Affecting Solution Formation	It's in Their Nature	Solubility and Temperature	Preparing and Diluting Solutions	Freezing Point Depression	Aloha Chemical Sunset	Solutions, Colloids, and Suspensions	Alka-Seltzer and Gas Solubility	Sorting Out Solutions	Instant Hand Warmers
Unifying Concepts and Processes										
Systems, order, and organization	✓	✓	✓	✓	✓	✓	✓	✓	✓	✓
Evidence, models, and explanation	✓	✓	✓	✓	✓	✓	✓	✓	✓	✓
Constancy, change, and measurement	✓	✓	✓	✓	✓	✓	✓	✓	✓	✓
Evolution and equilibrium	✓		✓				✓	✓		✓
Form and function	✓	✓								✓
Science as Inquiry										
Identify questions and concepts that guide scientific investigation	✓	✓	✓	✓	✓		✓	✓	✓	✓
Design and conduct scientific investigations	✓	✓	✓	✓	✓		✓	✓	✓	✓
Use technology and mathematics to improve scientific investigations			✓	✓	✓			✓		✓
Formulate and revise scientific explanations and models using logic and evidence	✓	✓	✓		✓		✓	✓	✓	✓
Recognize and analyze alternative explanations and models	✓	✓			✓				✓	✓
Communicate and defend a scientific argument	✓	✓	✓	✓	✓		✓	✓	✓	✓
Understanding scientific inquiry	✓	✓	✓	✓	✓	✓	✓	✓	✓	✓
Physical Science										
Structure of atoms										
Structure and properties of matter	✓	✓	✓	✓	✓	✓	✓	✓	✓	✓
Chemical reactions						✓				
Motions and forces										
Conservation of energy and the increase in disorder	✓		✓		✓	✓		✓	✓	✓
Interactions of energy and matter										✓

National Science Education Standards

Experiments and Demonstrations

Content Standards (continued)	Factors Affecting Solution Formation	It's in Their Nature	Solubility and Temperature	Preparing and Diluting Solutions	Freezing Point Depression	Aloha Chemical Sunset	Solutions, Colloids, and Suspensions	Alka-Seltzer and Gas Solubility	Sorting Out Solutions	Instant Hand Warmers
Science and Technology										
Identify a problem or design an opportunity										
Propose designs and choose between alternative solutions										
Implement a proposed solution										
Evaluate the solution and its consequences										
Communicate the problem, process, and solution										
Understand science and technology										
Science in Personal and Social Perspectives										
Personal and community health										
Population growth										
Natural resources										
Environmental quality									✓		
Natural and human-induced hazards									✓		
Science and technology in local, national, and global challenges						✓					
History and Nature of Science										
Science as a human endeavor										
Nature of scientific knowledge	✓	✓	✓	✓	✓		✓	✓	✓	✓
Historical perspectives										

Master Materials Guide

(for a class of 30 students working in pairs)

Experiments and Demonstrations

Chemicals	Flinn Scientific Catalog No.	Factors Affecting Solution Formation	It's in Their Nature	Solubility and Temperature	Preparing and Diluting Solutions	Freezing Point Depression	Aloha Chemical Sunset	Solutions, Colloids, and Suspensions	Alka-Seltzer and Gas Solubility	Sorting Out Solutions	Instant Hand Warmers
Alka-Seltzer® tablets	A0111								1		
Aluminum chloride, hexahydrate	A0026					210 g					
Ammonium hydroxide solution, 6 M	A0192								1 mL		
Benzoic acid	B0197		8 g								
Bromthymol blue indicator solution, 0.04% aqueous	B0173									10 mL	
Calcium chloride, dihydrate	C0015					210 g					
Cholesterol	C0179		8 g								
Cupric sulfate, pentahydrate, fine crystal	C0102	30 g			50 g						
Cupric sulfate, pentahydrate, medium crystal	C0105	3 g									
Cupric sulfate solution, 0.1 M	C0247								100 mL		
Dextrose	D0005		8 g								
Ethyl alcohol, anhydrous	E0007		225 mL								
Ethyl alcohol, 95%	E0009									150 mL	
Food coloring, dye set	V0003									optional	
Glycerin	G0019									50 mL	
Hexanes	H0046		255 mL								
Hydrochloric acid solution, 1 M	H0013							8 mL	25 mL		
Iodine	I0006		8 g								
Iodine-Potassium iodide solution	I0038								12 mL		
Potassium carbonate	P0038									85 g	
Potassium nitrate	P0070		8 g	45 g							
Sodium acetate, trihydrate	S0037										160 g
Sodium chloride	S0061					210 g					optional
Sodium hydroxide solution, 1 M	S0148								5 mL		
Sodium thiosulfate, pentahydrate	S0114						2 g		20 g		
Starch, potato, soluble	S0122								1 g		
Starch solution, 0.5%	S0151								130 mL		
Sucrose	S0134					210 g					
Toluene	T0019		100 mL								

Flinn ChemTopic™ Labs — Solubility and Solutions

Master Materials Guide

(for a class of 30 students working in pairs)

Experiments and Demonstrations

	Flinn Scientific Catalog No.	Factors Affecting Solution Formation	It's in Their Nature	Solubility and Temperature	Preparing and Diluting Solutions	Freezing Point Depression	Aloha Chemical Sunset	Solutions, Colloids, and Suspensions	Alka-Seltzer and Gas Solubility	Sorting Out Solutions	Instant Hand Warmers
Glassware											
Beakers											
50-mL	GP1005			7							
100-mL	GP1010	10									
250-mL	GP1020			7	15	60			3		
600-mL	GP1030							2		1	1
Erlenmeyer flasks											
125-mL	GP3040							6			
500-mL	GP3050										1
Funnel, short stem, fluted	GP5055							3			
Graduated cylinders											
10-mL	GP2005		15		15				1		
25-mL	GP2010	15				15	1		1		
100-mL	GP2020										1
Petri dish	GP3019							1			1
Stirring rod	GP5075	15			15	15			1		1
Test tubes											
13 × 100 mm	GP6063		90	45							
16 × 125 mm	GP6065					60					
20 × 150 mm	GP6068	45									
25 × 150 mm	GP6035								3		
Volumetric flasks with caps, 100-mL	GP4030				5					1	
General Equipment and Miscellaneous											
Balance, centigram (0.01-g precision)	OB2059	3		3	3	3			1		1
Bottles, plastic with cap	AP8962				15						
Colorimeter	TC1504				15						
Cuvettes	AP9149				75						
Dialysis tubing, 25 mm	AP4351							1			
Dialysis tubing clamps	FB1232							2			
Filter paper, qualitative, 15 cm	AP3105							3			
Funnel	AP3200				15						
Funnel support clamp	AP8222							1			
Gloves, heat-resistant	SE1031			7							1

Continued on next page

Master Materials Guide

(for a class of 30 students working in pairs)

Experiments and Demonstrations

General Equipment and Miscellaneous, Cont'd.	Flinn Scientific Catalog No.	Factors Affecting Solution Formation	It's in Their Nature	Solubility and Temperature	Preparing and Diluting Solutions	Freezing Point Depression	Aloha Chemical Sunset	Solutions, Colloids, and Suspensions	Alka-Seltzer and Gas Solubility	Sorting Out Solutions	Instant Hand Warmers
The Heat Solution™ Instant Hand Warmer	AP1933										1
Hot plate	AP4674	5		7			1		1		1
LabPro™ Interface System	TC1500			15							
Lens paper, book of 50 sheets	AP1141			1							
LoggerPro™ Software	TC1421			1							
Magnetic stirrer	AP6067									1	
Mortar and pestle	AP6066	5									
Pipets, Beral-type, graduated	AP1721		60	15	75			3			
Pipets, Beral-type, thin stem	AP1718								2		
Rubber stopper, size 2	AP2224	45									
Rubber stopper, size 5	AP2227								3		
Scissors, student	AP5394					1					
Spatula	AP8338	15	15	15	15						
Stir bar	AP5396									1	
Support stand	AP8226							1			
Test tube clamp	AP8217	15		15							
Test tube rack	AP1319	15	15		15				1		
Thermometer, digital	AP6049	15		15		15			1		1
Timer	AP8874	15									
Tongs, utility	AP1359										1
Tongue depressors	AP4412					30					
Wash bottle	AP1668		15		15						
Water, distilled or deionized	W0007, W0001	✓	✓	✓	✓	✓		✓		✓	✓
Wax pencil —or— Labeling tape	AP8291 AP1367			15	15						
Weighing paper —or— Weighing dishes	AP1121 AP1278	75		15						2	